Pilar

By
Pilar Beltran

A True American Story
As told to
Barbara Rich

PILAR

As told to BARBARA RICH

Copyright © 2016

ISBN 978-0-9969702-6-6

All rights reserved. No part of this publication may be reproduced, stored in a retrieval system, or transmitted in any form or by any means, electronic, mechanical, recording or otherwise, without the prior written permission of the author.

Published in the United States by
Five Birds Publications,
Laguna Woods, CA.

Five Bird System

This book is not intended as libelous, slanderous or to caste a negative pall on any person either living or dead. This is a first person memoir. Any opinions or statements made herein, therefore are the sole responsibility of the author.

Edited by Gordon Richiusa
Cover Design by Dana Stamos

PILAR

As told to BARBARA RICH

Pilar's

DEDICATION

I especially want to dedicate this book to the memory of my sister, Carmen and to my brother, Pedro who continues to be a source of strength and support for me.

PILAR

As told to BARBARA RICH

PREFACE
By The Writer

Hello everyone. I have to tell you about this book and how I came to be involved. My husband a writer, editor, and teacher, was approached by Pilar. She needed help with writing her life story because new memories had begun to unravel the mystery of her past and she wanted to commit the story to the page. After hearing the tale only briefly, my husband introduced Pilar to me. I realized that this was an opportunity to write something that not only would help an individual, but also might touch the hearts of many, many more men and women who have had to overcome terrible obstacles in life. We embarked on this task almost seven years ago. I will be forever grateful to Pilar for trusting me to write her incredible story.

I've learned an important lesson from my experience, which is, when it comes to exorcising demons, it doesn't matter how horrible they are, they can be defeated.

—Barbara Rich

PILAR

As told to BARBARA RICH

AUTHOR'S INTRODUCTION

Dear Reader,

I needed to write this book for myself, as a way to document my life to this point. Therapeutically it helped to open the locked passages to the window of my soul. For me the healing started when this book began. I am very grateful to Barbara Rich for her patience in expressing them in a way that could be shared. It has taken much more time than I expected for this project to be completed.

As is the case with suppressed emotions, the buried pain and experiences of my early life festered and polluted my present. I was unaware of the dynamic of these growing toxins, as they had contaminated every area of my life. Like a deep well of churning secrets, they awaited their chance to gush forth, into the light of day, raining down on all those who were nearby.

PILAR

It was the depth of the secrets held in my mind all those years that caused as much damage as the original wounds. I am learning that it is only by opening the wound and exposing it to the light and air, that I can heal and move toward a more sound and stable life. Please remember, my behaviors as described in this book were the result of deep, suppressed emotions, and not the rational, objective and calculated responses which some may have expected of me at the time. I apologize, in advance for anything, which may inadvertently shed a negative light on anyone else's behavior, either living or dead. That is not the intention of this book. As I begin my healing, I primarily am hoping that these pages might help to create a more positive life for those close to me. If anyone else can profit from my experiences that is even more gratifying.

--Pilar

As told to BARBARA RICH

Chapter Index

1. California, Sept.21 2009…　　　p.13

2. Colombia, S.A.1970…　　　p.35

3. Father Angel, Going to Colombia…　p.59

4. New York & Becoming American…　p.81

5. Pedro's Boyfriend…　　　p.115

6. All About John…　　　p.141

7. USA: Spring 1999/Summer 2000…　p.145

8. Pedro as Caretaker…　　　p.181

9. My In-laws…　　　p.189

10. My Parents…　　　p.195

11. Healing…　　　p.203

12. One Step Forward…　　　p.211

13. Photo Album…　　　p.245

PILAR

As told to BARBARA RICH

Chapter one
California, Sept 21, 2009

"*What have I done? What have I done?*"
I can clearly remember thinking this question to myself, with complete sincerity, as if I were having a perfectly normal conversation with someone else. The weird thing was that I also answered in the same way, "*What did I just do? I just dialed 911 and accused my husband of trying to kill me!*"

When I hung up the receiver and I knew, for certain that the call had really been made, something began nagging at my soul. Why was I questioning myself? I was not sure where reality began and my imagination ended. I felt as though I were two distinct and different people. One of *me* was outside of my body, looking impassively at the other as I went through the motions of dialing the three familiar, emergency numbers on the telephone. The *other me* was a wreck, a soul in complete panic and turmoil. With each button that was pushed, the unfamiliar deeply hidden *me* took a stronger hold of the *me* that was acting, and at the surface. I had observed myself losing control to a wild anger that was out of synch with the observer *me*. I did not know the *me* that I was observing. I did not like the hidden, angry and irrational me who had suddenly taken control of my physical body, but the familiar part of me that was being pushed aside and was not the observer, was powerless to alter my actions.

"Hello, 911 what is your emergency?"
"My husband is trying to kill me."
"Where is your husband right now?"
"He's in the other room. He has a gun. You need to come quickly and arrest him, now! Please!"

I omitted the fact that my husband was actually standing only a few feet away. It did not seem important at the time. In fact, nothing (including the reason why I'd called the police to begin with) seemed to be affecting me in any way at that moment. I was very calmly and instantly responding to the questions and directions being posed to me.

"A car has been dispatched already. Is there anyone else in the house with you?"
"You mean, besides my husband?"

As told to BARBARA RICH

"Yes," the dispatcher was also keeping her cool. *"Yes, besides you and your husband."*

"Yes, my two daughters. He threatened to kill me, and them, as soon as I go to sleep. I need help! We're in danger."

"Where is your husband right now?"

"He is nearby, in the house."

This bit of information seemed to set the wheels of motion spinning much more quickly.

"Listen carefully. As soon as you hang up, get your children and leave the house immediately. Police are on the way. There is a patrol car in your neighborhood. Do you understand? Get out of the house immediately. The police will be there in less than one minute."

I tossed the phone back into its cradle and turned briefly to see my husband's face. He looked like a cartoon caricature of a man in total shock and disbelief. His mouth hung open, literally. The call had been precipitated by that moment of clarity I talked about. Some might say I had snapped, which is probably closer to the truth. But, at the time, everything seemed so clear. I had acted as if there was no alternative to what I had just done. It was simply a matter

PILAR

of life and death for both my two beautiful daughters and me. I cannot remember running down the hallway to my daughters' shared room, or waking and dressing them, but it must have been done at an incredible speed. We ran outside the garage door. The cops came as soon as possible.

The hands on the clock in the kitchen had not moved, it seemed, but I still had time for one more call to my friend, Carla. I had taken her home number, because I had recently told her that I suspected that my husband was plotting to do harm to the girls and me.

"Are you sure that you are in danger?" She had asked.

I said that I was. She told me to call her if anything developed. I thought that maybe this fell into that category. I told her what I had done and said and why I had made the first call and she supported me in my decision, based upon what I said. We hung up and I waited for the police to arrive. So much had happened, but it was in the blink of an eye. My husband had not moved. He sat impassively, stunned like a man who had just seen a horrible accident and was in shock.

As told to BARBARA RICH

On the surface, it had been a night like any other, except that I knew my husband had been having an affair, or affairs and was growing further and further away from our children and me. So, when I say that it was a night like any other, I mean that I was trying to make it seem that way...up until the time that I apparently snapped.

I couldn't take it anymore. For some reason I believed that it was not only my right, but my *duty* to make him suffer for what he did—even though I did not know exactly what it was that he had done--but I never believed it would come to this, or that I was even capable of such an act. Even at the time, I did not realize that the 911 call was truly a call for help, which would save me from dangers that had been suppressed and brewing below the surface for many years.

Two days prior to this life-changing phone call, I had discovered that my husband had left his email on his home-office computer open when he'd gone away for the day. Some might say that it was wrong to look at the messages that were still open there, but others—and now I'm one of them—agree that often a cheater leaves such messages in more ways than this. The aggrieved spouse usually does not want to read the messages or "see the signs" of infidelity. Women, and some men I supposed, just look the other way, or "turn off the screen" not really wanting to know that their loved-one is being unfaithful. That's not what I did in this case. I sat at the desk and read the open message. Then, I began a search of all the old messages with the same or similar headings.

What I discovered after only a few minutes of sober observation was a series of liaisons, which had been going on for years without my knowledge. My stunned amazement gave quickly way to a sense of purpose.

While I sat there and read, the phone rang. My husband was calling from work asking if he could have a salad for dinner that evening. I did not let on that I'd read his emails, or had seen his credit card statements and knew that he was seeing at least one other woman.

"A salad?" I thought to myself. "He must be trying to lose weight for his girlfriend." I knew he was not concerned with how I perceived him.

As told to BARBARA RICH

Our sex life had slowly diminished over the years. I felt like Mother Teresa, living celibate, after the birth of our last child. I was still young and fully engaged in trying to make myself appealing to my husband. I wanted intimacy, but he seemed to be losing interest, no matter what I tried.

I had entered therapy about three years before this in an attempt at salvaging some self-esteem and making sense of my fears and anxiety. None of these previous sessions involved my husband, but were exclusively for my own benefit.

My therapist and I had tried at first to get John to attend sessions, but eventually the marriage counseling had become my own personal growth activity. This was probably the first ignored sign. Slowly our sessions began to pinpoint an underlying, low-self-esteem problem. John was eventually ignored as a subject of conversation and questions like, "*What can you do for yourself?*" became more prevalent in our sessions.

I should have really suspected sooner what was going on with my husband, as soon as when he took a sudden interest in his physical condition and was trying to "lose weight and get in shape."

This request for a salad was like an insult that I was not going to let go unchallenged. How should I react? What could I do that would turn the tables to my advantage?

I decided to make him a salad like one he'd never had before, and would probably never want again.

"I've got a special recipe I've been meaning to try," I told him.

"Oh great, Hon," he said. *"I'm looking forward to it."*

Before he got home, I systematically began to collect the ingredients for my special recipe. I took some carrots from the refrigerator, cut them into thin slices and I marinated them for four hours with urine-tainted water that I scooped from my daughter's toilet! The girls were forever forgetting to flush, so I knew that the marinade was going to be there when I needed it.

I then found a suitable cucumber and lifting my skirt I inserted it into my vagina. I made sure that the vegetable was properly coated at both ends and then cut and sliced everything nicely onto a special plate. When he got home, I served him the *special salad* on a plate that had been drying in the sun on a paper plate. Later I transferred the concoction to a regular plate so as to avoid detection.

The girls and I had a similar, but untainted version of the meal on separate plates. There was no suspicion from anyone that Daddy's salad was *more special* than what was on our plates.

"Hon," he always called me Hon, *"This salad tastes funny,"* John said after only one bite.

"What's funny about it?" My oldest daughter, asked. I did not have to feign confusion. She was merely being honest. Her salad tasted fine.

"It's a strange taste, kind of like vinegar."

"It's a Spanish sauce I've been thinking about trying. Maybe you just don't like the peppers," I said. What I was thinking was, EAT MY SHIT!

"Well, it's not that bad. I appreciate the effort you put into it." He was polite and cleaned his plate.

PILAR

After dinner everyone had gone their separate ways in the roomy, tastefully decorated house and I drifted into a fog that was made of anger and something else I couldn't quite picture. I poured myself a glass of wine and watched television while trying to unwind. I have no idea what show was on, because my attention was turned inward. I was trying to focus on the loathing and hatred that was building inside. With each sip of wine, the anger and hurt was building and becoming clear. Suddenly, everything outside my anger became non-existent. With sudden purpose I thought to myself. "That's it. Enough is enough!"

I did not know when I started the seemingly endless walk from the living room to the office, what I was planning on doing. I was driven, but still just watching. I only knew that I could not stand another minute in the house with my husband. I found my prey in the second room that my hunt had taken me, our bedroom. He was asleep.

I stood at the doorway, looking inside, and saw him lying on the bed with the tool of his downfall, the laptop nearby.

As told to BARBARA RICH

In a voice that was brewing with emotion just below the surface I woke him rudely with the words, *"Get the fuck out!"*

Startled, my husband looked like a young animal encountering a potential danger for the first time, both worried and confused. *"What are you talking about, Hon? Are you O.K.?"*

"I know you've been fucking around," I said in that same, living-dead monotone. *"I know what you've been doing and that you've been doing it for a long time. I know that you don't really care about me, or the girls. I want you out of here, tonight. Now!"*

"You're not serious. You've been angry with me before and you'll get over it."

"Aren't you even going to try to lie to me? Aren't you even going to try and deny it for a moment?"

He was silent in his guilt. This enraged me even more, though it wouldn't have mattered what he did or said. I was obviously focused on this one goal. There was nothing he could do or say that would have altered my actions now.

"I am not putting up with this for another minute. I'm done," I added. *"If you*

don't leave here right now, I'm calling 911 and have you thrown in jail!"

This threat of jail really got his attention and he too went momentarily on automatic pilot.

Standing and facing me defiantly, he yelled, *"You're pathetic! No one will believe you are in danger from me. This is my house, not yours. You'd never do something stupid like that, something that would ruin your life as well as mine, especially in front of the girls."*

Since he was now facing me in close proximity, I did the only thing that I felt I could do, something I felt that he had earned. I spit in his face like a street girl in Colombia. Only slightly shocked, he continued to smugly protest in his, so called, commanding voice of reason.

I walked to the telephone and began to dial the call that I had just threatened. He was stunned and, as I said, literally had his mouth hanging open. Slowly, I could see a little fear creeping into his expression and somehow I felt that he was finally getting *exactly what he deserved*.

Now, with the police on their way I moved methodically again, this time for the

As told to BARBARA RICH

children, and as I did I walked down the hall and noticed the gun—which I just had reported was being used against me--was still in the locked-box, on a shelf high in a closet where the children could not get to it.

This is an important point: When I had spoken to the 911 Operator I wasn't merely trying to think of a story that would get him out of my house. *I truly believed what I had been saying.* The image of the gun-box, on the shelf did not register with my current reality. Reality was far removed from the place where I was operating, that at the time, the image on the gun did not register. Somehow, I convinced myself that I hadn't just made up the story, but that I was really in danger.

I felt I had to protect myself, and especially my two girls from a very real threat, their father. My fear was directed at my lying, cheating husband. A scattering of thoughts were racing in my mind while I tried to piece together what was happening, in between shouting obscenities and accusations at my husband while carrying and guiding my two daughters through the back door and into the garage.

PILAR

I wanted him to at least have compassion, ask for forgiveness or feel or pretend to feel remorse. He was cold as ice. Not even an, "I'm sorry, Pilar. Can you forgive me?" No. Nada. Nunca.

His measured, yet understandable reaction just increased my wrath towards him. I wanted to punish him at that moment. It seemed like *justice* for endless, unspeakable abuses.

Entering the girls room, gathering their things and heading for the back door must have taken place in the blink of an eye. Before I knew what had happened, the garage door was rising. We could see uniformed legs of one of the officers. My husband was standing next to the girls and me, almost as if we were on a way to a family outing.

"Did you call 911?" Two police officers were standing next to the garage, when the door rose. One was standing to the side, his hand on his holstered weapon.

"Yes, my husband threatened to kill me and my children as soon as I go to sleep." I remember saying *my children,* not *our children.*

"Is this the man with the weapon?" Asked the ready but relaxed officer.

"Yes, there's a gun but it's inside." I took them to the closet and showed them the box.

My husband made no attempt to resist. He was as dumbfounded as the girls and I. He merely stayed with the second officer. They probably knew one another, but did not acknowledge that fact.

"Anyone else in the house?"

"No one else is here."

"Are you girls alright?" The second officer spoke directly to them now.

You could see the concern on John's face as well and he spoke directly to them, *"Stay with your mother. Everything will be alright."*

My husband begged the police to spare my arrest considering my hysterical state of mind, and no one was arrested at that time. John did leave however, and spent about a week on our nearby, small sailboat which we kept in a close harbor.

I returned to the house and turned my attention to consoling the girls. I felt that I had just saved them from a terrible fate. We huddled together on my bed. Sleep was evasive, but eventually came.

PILAR

The next day, upon awakening my mind was flooded again with the events of the night before. My daughters asked very few questions, but I'm sure they had no idea what they had just witnessed. They only knew, what they had seen and heard and that I believed we were all in danger because of their father. They trusted me entirely, and were forced in an instant to choose between their parents. They chose to trust me more than they trusted their own father.

While my mind was racing I awoke amazingly refreshed, as if a huge stone had been lifted from my shoulders. I was very methodical and controlled as if I was the legal and professional authority, not my husband. I couldn't help smiling, thinking that my husband would have been impressed with the way I was handling the process. After the girls went reluctantly to school, I went straight to the business at hand. It was like adding ingredients to a salad.

I knew, for instance, that I needed to get a restraining order to keep him away from me. I used the laptop that I'd found the letters on to start preparing a statement. The anger had festered so, I was ready to explode but the writing of the accusation seemed to relieve the internal pressure. As the pressure lessened, I was less repulsed at the touch of the computer, which I probably associated with dirty sex.

Before the girls were halfway finished with school, the document was complete. I got into the family car—*family*, I thought, that's ironic--and drove to the local courthouse. Then went to the bank and emptied our safe deposit box. I took all the money from the checking and saving accounts and left him fifty cents on each.

I had been to the courthouse many times before. This was the place where John did most of his work. As an attorney we had met here many times between court appearances. Often I brought the girls there, or carried over a sack lunch. It seemed somehow fitting that I was now here now to beat him at his own game.

Still I felt that my actions not only were necessary, but actually somehow *righteous*. My husband had been with another woman. How could he? I felt like a fool. My heart screamed for a completely out of proportion vengeance. I wanted him to pay for what he had done, and, in the back of my mind, I couldn't get rid of the

PILAR

thought that I had somehow saved my daughters from a very real danger, as well.

The clerk who took my petition recognized me, and my last name, but apparently was not too shocked. He had probably seen many of the judge's, police officers and lawyer's spouses here, under similar circumstances. Divorce is high in the U.S., but it is especially high for those in the criminal justice system.

"If you want to see the judge today, I have an opening in one hour," the clerk said dryly.

"Yes, please. This is urgent," I told him, with conviction, then realized that every plaintiff probably felt the same way.

When the judge saw my petition, he read it through and seeing the statement of danger, the 911 call and the potential for harm to the children, he granted my request for a safety perimeter of 1000 feet.

"Because of the seriousness of this matter, I am setting a hearing date in three days. You and your husband will appear and we'll determine how Social Services and the Criminal Court should become involved."

"Thank you Your Honor."

As told to BARBARA RICH

It was all so incredibly easy. Because of the thoroughness of the petition, there was no hesitation in granting me my every request. I knew that I was one step closer to putting John away for a long time, and believed that this was going to make my whole family much safer. It was only the first step, but an important one in making my claims seem more valid. I knew that in the end, it was really only my word against his.

Perhaps for all the wrong reasons, therefore, as soon as I was done in court I went to my church to talk to the pastor. I had been raised a Catholic, but had chosen to change my church when I had left my family home and come to the United States. Even though I had only a vague memory of the rituals and procedures I could not help but feel like I was making a confession, even though we were sitting in a very business-like office.

"Pilar, I am sorry that you have been put through this, but I have to ask some questions. Are you sure that John is really a danger to you? To the girls? I cannot see him ever hurting any of you. How did you find out about the affair? Have you talked to John since

the arrest? Have you been having sexual relations with John up until now? Are you going to a doctor to be checked?"

This last question caught my attention out of all the rest.

"Checked? Checked for what?"

"Sexually transmitted diseases. If John has been having unprotected sex elsewhere—and you haven't told me otherwise—then you may need to make sure you haven't been infected...with anything."

I realized suddenly what the pastor was referring to...STDs or worse, A.I.D.S. and HIV. While still sitting in the church office, I called my doctor and made an appointment. It was getting late, so I wouldn't be able to see the doctor until the next day. But, before the girls got out of school, I could go to the lab and have my blood drawn. The doctor would send an order for H.I.V. and other STD screenings to the lab immediately.

Now I needed help with my growing anxiety. I stopped by the therapist's office and told her the story of the hell I had been going through.

Susan, my therapist for several months calmed me. She repeated the often-voiced mantras that, I had to take care of myself, and that she would be there for me if I needed her, anytime. I felt so relieved and comforted knowing she would be there to help, as if I'd never heard those words before that moment. She may have been just trying to be responsible, or perhaps was reacting to something I may have said in an earlier session, but before I left she asked, in the same tone as the pastor, "Are you *sure* about all this?"

Two days later I spoke to another friend named John, a dear friend of my husband and me for many years. We talked for hours about my fears and suspicions and he echoed Susan's and my pastor's concerns.

"Pilar, Pilar, do you understand the consequences of your actions?" His question was pointed, but redirected my attention away from John. *"Child Services will mark the girls' lives forever."*

"Oh...my...God!" The measured phrasing of these words came out of the very center of my soul. *"What have I done?"*

My children! I could never harm my children. Hadn't I done this for their sake? And, there was something else that continued to nag at me. Why *was* I doing this?

For all his faults—real or imagined in my current state--to threaten me, or my daughters was not like John. It was completely out of character. And what about the gun? Wasn't it in the box when I showed it to the police? How did he get it back in there when he'd been right next to me most of the time? Could I really remember John threatening me, or the girls, or even suggesting that I was going to be harmed?

I could not get a clear image in my head of when I'd seen the gun, how he'd used it to intimidate me, or what had happened to make me feel threatened. Somehow, though, I had a clear memory of my life being threatened by a gun. Wasn't it that one? Was *that* the gun? Was John the danger, or was it someone else? But who?

Other questions hit me like rocks thrown at my forehead. *Had I lied?* Why would I do such a thing?

I began to allow the possibility that I'd imagined it to creep into my mind. Was I hallucinating from jealousy? What was wrong with me? Was I completely insane or is this how people are supposed to feel when there is an emotional trauma in their lives?

"Oh my God, Oh my God." The words started pouring from me as if I were chanting, like a prayer of forgiveness for a sin I was not sure who had committed. I was feeling frantic at the thought of what I must have done of what I HAD done! I was frightened that I, Pilar could have told such a story. *But, was it a lie, a sin, if I had believed it?*

It didn't matter right now. I had to continue to relinquish this burden that had been weighing upon me.

It was so out of character for me. I am usually a very controlled person, the realization came from my lips like words someone else was saying. *"I lied! I lied! I made the whole story up. John never threatened us! What am I going to do?"*

My friend continued his cross-examination very carefully to determine which parts of the story had been based on truth. Yes, my husband was having an affair. Yes, he had been having sex with other women for years, but how had I related this problem to the safety of my daughters? I did not know at that

PILAR

moment. I only knew that I had been to court and my husband had been accused of a felony...by me.

"Pilar, " My friend said soothingly, *"It is not too late. You can fix this. Call the court and admit what you've done. Tell the truth immediately and have this case dismissed. Don't get involved with Child Services."*

My eyes were suddenly opened as to what I must be prepared to do and together we outlined a step-by-step strategy of my next moves. It would be difficult to unmake the mess I'd created, but not impossible.

For the next two days I was frantically calling again, the police, my lawyer, the pastor, friends, neighbors, the therapist, anyone I had spoken to previously to retract my story about my plight and especially the 911 call.

John was an asshole, perhaps. Certainly he had problems with keeping his dick in the relationship where it belonged, but he was not the threat that I had accused him of being. Daughters need a good father, and any father who was performing fatherly duties with love and kindness, even a philanderer, was better than no father at all. Somehow, I knew this one thing above all others.

As told to BARBARA RICH

I was wearing down because nothing about undoing what I'd done was easy, emotionally or otherwise. After checking off the important contacts list, my follow up call was to Susan, my therapist. She had been earning her money lately. I made an appointment to see her that afternoon. She wasted no time getting me to face the urgency of my responsibilities.

"You have to put things right with your husband, for your children's sake." She advised me. She knew this was not going to be easy given my fragile state of mind, but it was the court that I was dealing with, and my husband's reputation and of course his relationship with our daughters.

"You have to take care of all this right away," she said emphatically.

"Where should I begin?"

"Pilar, simply go back to those people you lied to and tell them the truth! Start with your pastor, before going to the court. This will give you a chance to tell your new story, in person, without legal consequences. But, please don't stop there. No matter what happens with your church, you must go to court and clear your husband of the charges you've made against him. This is the most important thing you can do."

"Even though he cheated on me?"

"That's not what you are accusing him of doing. He will have to accept responsibility for what he's done to you and to your relationship with him, but that doesn't include threatening your life."

"What do you think will happen to me?" I asked with a sigh, now beginning to see how crazy and reactionary I had been behaving.

"It doesn't matter. The truth may not set you free, but it is your only option at this point. It has very little to do with you or with John. It's your daughters I am thinking about. They need their father, especially if he has been good to and with them. They also need their mother, but only if she is willing to act unselfishly on their behalf."

Naturally, she was absolutely right. It would be better for me to go to jail admitting my false accusations, then to lose the trust and respect of my daughters completely, while holding onto a lie.

The girls were both at school, so I dressed quickly and headed straight for our church. The pastor was a family friend. He seemed to truly love both John and myself equally and was completely baffled when I had originally accused my husband of trying to kill me, and threatening the girls.

I burst into the pastor's office after calling and pleading for an immediate audience. I flung the door open so abruptly that a blast of air nearly blew a stack of papers off of the pastor's desk. He looked somewhat frightened, based I suspected on what I'd told him the last time I was in his office, only two days before this.

"What is it, Pilar? What's so urgent?"

"Pastor, I lied." I decided to blurt it out and get it over with.

"When did you lie? Which part?"

"All of it, except what I believed. I made it up, the part about John threatening the girls and me. He was cheating. That part is true, but we are in no danger. He would never do anything to physically harm us."

"I know that. What do you mean, *except what I believed*?"

"That's why I'm here, Pastor. I had to tell somebody first, and I thought it might as well be you."

PILAR

I went on to give him a brief report of my whole life, up until that moment, including a hidden realization that my sister had been sexually assaulted right in front of me, which we both brushed right past. Thoughts continued to form words that spilled out of my mouth which I had no previous conscious memory of thinking.

He was very patient and understanding and it didn't take a degree in psychology to understand that what I had accused John of doing, directly related to my own ancient and suppressed history. On the other hand, it is never easy to have to tell your pastor or anyone else in authority that you have lied to them.

"I'm glad you are coming forward now that you understand what really happened," he said at last. "Regardless of how things turn out in your marriage, and certainly you have been wronged in the eyes of God by your husband's infidelity, you can only take charge of your own actions. You have to recant your testimony, as soon as possible."

We agreed that I should not wait any longer; since I was motivated to amend my story right way, I left the pastor's office and headed straight for the court. Changing my testimony was not as easy or precise as my original accusation had been. My actions, in the original accusation had been part of a methodical plan, with some understanding of how the legal system worked.

Here, I was basically going into court to accuse myself of perjury, a crime I knew that was more serious, in many cases than the crime that was originally under consideration.

We really don't like dishonesty in this country. After all, wasn't lying at the core of my problems with John? Wasn't that the real reason why I was even contemplating a divorce in the first place?

A special hearing was called just prior to the original hearing to allow my husband to plead to the charges I'd leveled against him. Everyone, including John was in the courtroom when I stood up to face the hearing judge. She was the same one I'd convinced to grant me a restraining order and to charge my husband with assault. She glanced at the note handed to her by the bailiff that outlined the purpose of this "pre" hearing, then looked up at me with piercing, yet familiar eyes. It was, as if she'd heard it all before and was not going to be shocked now.

PILAR

"So, you want to recant?" she asked with a stunned stare.

"Yes, your honor."

"You no longer feel that your life is threatened?"

"No."

"Maybe you could have your client," the judge was talking to my lawyer now "explain to me why I should not charge her with perjury."

"The Prosecution would like to state for the record that we will not press charges in this matter." This was probably a first for the judge as well. The prosecutor against John, and potentially against me was answering for *my* lawyer, who had now become representation for the defense.

Everyone, including John had been contacted prior to this moment. My lawyer had made it clear that he was willing to make this a very public and messy affair if anyone wanted to make an example of me. It was particularly embarrassing to stand before the exact same judge to admit that I had lied.

I was still savvy enough to obtain a real lawyer at this point. I could think of at least two laws I'd broken which might lead to the very real possibility that I would now be sent to jail. The court does not look kindly on perjury, under any circumstances, especially when 911 is brought into the crime.

"*You are here again, with your husband to retract your claims. What prompted this reversal Mrs. Beltran?*" The judge gave me one last chance to convince her to spare me jail time.

"*I have no excuse or explanation, Your Honor. All I can say is that, I must have snapped. I was so angry with my husband when I found out about his affair that I acted without thinking. I am truly sorry. I'm ashamed. I'm still confused. This is not like me, Your Honor, but it is also not like my husband either. He should not be kept from his children. He has been a good father and none of us are in danger, I realize that now.*"

"*Should I believe you now, or should I believe you before when you said you were telling the truth?*"

"*I am telling the truth, now. If you look at the arresting report, I showed the arresting officers the gun I believed was being used against me, was still locked in the hall closet when they arrived. It did not occur to me to change my story, because I did not realize until now that I had made the whole thing up."*

"*Case dismissed!*" The judge took pity on me and, while dropping the charges against John only suggested that I seek even more intensive counseling. He had no idea what good advice that was!

John had moved into a small apartment near the beach and went straight there to wait for me to be able to talk to him about our problems. I needed to bolster my nerves and understand my actions better, before I would be able to talk to him. Even though I knew that I did not want to be married to him anymore, I was not sure exactly what I DID want.

I went about my daily routine, remarkably at ease for someone who had just barely missed being sent to prison and who had just had her life completely turned upside down by her husband's admission of multiple affairs—not to mention an apparent psychotic break.

Then, something else occurred which put my reaction into the proper perspective, and made sense of the off-hand comment to the pastor about my sister's rape.

As told to BARBARA RICH

I was standing at the kitchen sink. Washing the breakfast dishes after the girls had been dropped off at school. I vividly remember the morning sun shining on the large-basin sink like a spotlight on a stage. It seemed to be lighting a path to the back roads of my mind, a scene that I recognized from somewhere far away, in the past.

Suddenly my face shifted from placidly calm to a mask of horror! I gasped and remember my knees buckling beneath me, as I fell to the floor. I looked up from the sink and stared at the light shining in from the window like it was God's messenger shining directly at my soul. I suddenly realized the reason why I had concocted the story about my husband!

The problems and the dangers of a philandering spouse and sexual addict didn't only relate directly to *me*, but went much deeper than my current situation.

I remembered. I remembered. I remembered vividly, exactly what had happened!

PILAR

As told to BARBARA RICH

Chapter two
Colombia, South America, 1970

"Carmen y Pilar ve al cuarto de tu padre que el quiere veros, neccesita que le masagen los pies."

As I knelt on the floor, I held onto the side of the sink in desperation. It was as if my grip and the feel of cold porcelain was the only thing keeping me from totally disintegrating. I raised my eyes slowly and slightly and was struck by such a vivid impression of deja vu and insight, all rolled into one, that I had completely lost track of the present situation and was immersed in the past.

The height of my gaze took me back to a younger time in my life. From where I now slumped, I was at about the same height as I would have been at age eight when living with my family in Colombia. In my mind I was clearly picturing my mother standing at the large-basined sink, exactly in dimension to the one I had installed in my current home. I had never realized this similarity before this moment. She was a very beautiful woman in her day, but she had lost her luster by this time in my life. My mother's image turned to me as she had many times and was giving my sister and I casual direction to attend to my father in his bedroom.

"Carmen and Pilar," she called, *"Your father is waiting for his foot massage."*

As had happened countless times, Papa would already be in the bedroom of our modest home in Colombia. There were only seven rooms that were situated around the large kitchen. The sink in that kitchen faced the outdoors, which you could see through a small window. The sink was shaped like a tub.

That similarity, my current problems with my husband, and the angle of my view had combined to launch me backward even further in time as if I were reliving the moment. It was not a *mere* memory or really a memory of any kind that I was used to having, because there were details that had never surfaced prior to this moment. It was perhaps the coming together of the past and present with my husband that bridged those moments that had before been left isolated.

My mother's direction to give the foot massage was a common occurrence. I was only seven and did not question why it took two of us to do the job or why my mother was always the bearer of this news.

Carmen was eleven but she was fully developed already, like a young woman. Her breasts were round and firm, her shape voluptuous even by adult standards. We both looked like our mother in many ways, but somehow, as similar as we were there was also differences.

My sister had been blessed with a countenance some call *angelic*, a special quality that attracts. It had been the cause for many problems for her in school. Ten and eleven year olds are just not supposed to be that well endowed. Often, when we walked home from school together men would call and whistle from worksites or their cars. We both knew they were whistling at Carmen, not at me.

In school she had to endure the usual taunting that young girls who develop early are subject to, and by adolescent boys who had not developed any self esteem or confidence. In addition she drew more than casual attention from the adults who were supposed to be caring for us. At the time, I did not realize the depth of the insensitive remarks some would make, or the catcalls and animal growls. Carmen was seemingly impervious to the attention and acted like none of it really mattered.

When we were called into massage Papa, I seemed to be the only one who ever actually touched his feet but we were both called upon to do this duty. We siblings had established close ties on our trip from Spain to Colombia, so I did not think it was strange to be ordered to accompany her, even though she seemed to be in charge. It was the same for all three of us. Whenever one of us was given a chore, often another sibling assumed that they were getting the assignment as well.

I look back on it now and realize that my sister was probably protecting me in a way on those walks to and from school, since I was so much younger, undeveloped and kind of a tomboy. Whenever men got out of hand, she would always be the one to gather their attentions rather than me. Later in life, circumstance changed that.

But here I was, kneeling on the floor and stunned by this scene, realizing the impact that my family history had on my life, and how it had influenced my reaction to my husband's infidelity. We are all, in the end only the sum

As told to BARBARA RICH

total of our experiences and our reactions to them. When children are not given the opportunity to grow up and flourish with a family's support, they look for other ways to fill their needs. Everyone has to decide for oneself how to interpret and to cope with the challenges of life. And, in some cases, coping means completely blocking out giant chunks of memories.

    We had gone to Colombia, by way of freighter. This was not my first voyage. I had been once before in the belly of my mother. She was pregnant with me when she had traveled both to and from South America and I have always believed that this has contributed to my love of the ocean.

    "Vayamos!" Angel, my father shouted, as they boarded an Italian ship, the Virginia. Carmen, my brother, Pedro and I scrambled to catch up with my father. My eyes were wide and curious at the site of this huge boat, which must have seemed much larger to us children than it did to the adults.

    The reason we were traveling on a ship that was primarily a cargo freighter was because my dad knew it was much cheaper for an entire family to travel this way, rather than a

PILAR

pleasure cruiser. It was not just my family that he had to transport, but all our furnishings and belongings.

We were leaving Barcelona, Spain on our way to Colombia, South America. For me, it was an adventure. I remember walking along the gangplank when we boarded and noticing the height of the railing of the ship. It was just a little too high for me to see over. I would have to nestle onto the stairways to view the ocean, which I often did on that month long journey.

I can still picture the details of the small flecks of rusted grey paint the covered the entire freighter, and can smell the mixture of diesel fuel and salt water. Even today, when I am sailing and under wind power, there lingers in the clean smell of the sea a memory of fuel and sometimes, even paint.

There were several crewmembers whose sole job was to continuously repair the paint and varnish of the ship. On the water, rust is a constant threat. Everything was made of metal it seemed, except for a few handrails where the captain and other important crew would slide down when they had to move quickly.

As told to BARBARA RICH

The captain was a nice gentleman, but he could be frightening to a young girl. Maybe it was the uniform, his great weight, or his heavy beard. I made this journey two times, once in each direction spending a total of two months on board this ship. I don't know if there were only a few vessels making the journey in those days, or if my father had chosen this ship for some other reason.

Each crossing took about a month, as we stopped in many ports to deliver cargo along the way. I am sure that my father saved a great deal of money by us traveling this way, but I am also certain that these trips are reasons why I still feel most at home when I'm on the sea. The accommodations were comfortable, but there were very few passengers.

Although the age difference between my sister and I was only three years, I spent more time with my brother, Pedro who was much older. We were very close. At least that is how it seemed. It also appeared that my brother and sister never really got along. They were always fighting, especially later in life, but on board a ship we were forced by necessity to tighten our bonds. Pedro, a teenaged boy was tall and handsome with flowing locks of hair and piercing eyes. He always seemed to be smiling and happy.

"Pilar, where are you? Come out now! Pilar, Pilar, I can't find you." Pedro shouted throughout the ship, as he searched for me while playing hide and seek.

I was giggling as I hid in a cabinet in the galley.

"Where is she? Where could she have gone?" I heard someone else say. My family knew I was a very mischievous child, always seeking adventure. I thought to myself, *I really found the best place to hide. They will never find me.*

Carmen, Pedro and I had started an official hide-and-seek several hours before this. I had not seen either of them for quite some time and may have fallen asleep in my hiding place for a short period. When I woke there seemed to be a lot of commotion. Everyone had gotten involved in the game somehow. There was an unusual amount of activity, which I could only catch a glimpse of through the small horizontal slits in the door of the cabinet where I was hidden.

As told to BARBARA RICH

There were just too many people involved in the search, so I wondered, "What is going on?"

Now, I noticed that loud sirens and alarm bells were also accompanying the search. Unless everyone had gotten in on the game, there was no reason for this. Then an officer came into the galley with my father, mother and two siblings. My curiosity got the best of me and I began to peek out from the cabinet very slowly. I was now focused on my family and had forgotten the game altogether.

At first I did not make any connection with myself to the conversation I was hearing. "She may have fallen overboard," my father was telling the crewmate. "You must stop the ship!"

"Yes, sir. The captain has called for a full stop. We're in the process of searching the ship now. It's possible but unlikely that she has fallen out of a portal or over the rail. If we must we will turn the vessel about if we cannot find your daughter onboard."

They then launched into a detailed discussion about how difficult it was to turn a ship, even a moderately sized one, around on the open seas.

PILAR

"It can take up to half an hour. And, even if we do stop we will have traveled far. I've never seen anyone fall overboard, but I've heard stories and the victims are never found. There are currents and each person would drift at a different rate. In fact, if a small child had fallen overboard there was very little chance for survival. Does your daughter know how to swim?"

That question was rhetorical. No child could have survived an overboard fall and besides, I did *not* know how to swim.

Suddenly I realized what was happening. They were all looking for *me* and *had*, in fact *not* joined our game of hide and seek! I knew I was going to get into trouble, but I decided it was better to pop out immediately than to keep hiding.

"I'm here!" I shouted as jumped up, nearly knocking my mother into a faint, like a vision of someone who had come back from the dead.

There was both a sense of relief and anger with everyone concerned. My father didn't know whether to hug me or spank me. He did both.

As told to BARBARA RICH

Until that time, my mother had been hiding in our cabin, beside herself with grief. Carmen and Pedro were both assisting in the search by showing the crewmembers where our usual hiding places had been, while my father had basically taken complete charge of the search.

I later learned that it was my father--with some strong arguments and challenges to the captain--who had convinced the captain to stop the ship and bring it about. The captain wanted to exhaust all other possibilities before performing this difficult and mostly pointless maneuver. It was one of the very few times that he had to my memory, expressed his concern for my wellbeing, or the wellbeing of any of his children or wife. When it came to Papa's needs, wants and desires...only Papa mattered.

After my spankings and hugs from all my family members, my father and I had to go and face the captain together. The two of them standing side-by-side were a very imposing force, especially to a little girl, and it was made clear that I should find some other form of entertainment for the remainder of the trip. With alligator tears in my eyes, I begged forgiveness and mercy and vowed never again to act the way I had acted, even though I was unsure exactly what I had done differently than either Pedro or Carmen. It was only hide and seek. Why had they gotten so angry?

In the end, partly because we were forced into it, this became a time when my siblings and I became very close. Because our physical activity was limited, we turned to making up games in our heads. It got so that we could almost read each other's thoughts. These periods of closeness and sustained concentration on one another lasted far into our adulthood and may have been the catalyst for many more of our individual decisions than I fully realize, even to this day.

As told to BARBARA RICH

Chapter three
Father Angel, & Going to Colombia.

The reason we were going to Colombia was to be with my mother's family. My father's family was from Spain and now I was going to see my maternal, South American relatives. The Spanish are envied in many American cultures. Colombia is no exception. My father had the classic features of a Spaniard with strong lean physique and blue Spanish eyes. This probably worked to his advantage in many ways while we lived in Colombia.

Before we left Spain my father was partners in a trucking company and worked on the streets. I found out later that he had feared we were going broke, which had prompted our sudden departure from Spain. He had invested heavily in the prospect that a new road would be built and that his trucks would be in high demand. Unexpectedly, he was told that the road would be postponed for a decade and maybe not be built at all. If the road was not going to be open, he decided that he was destined for bankruptcy. Without warning, or any discussion he put everything into his partner's name and we left without telling anyone where we were going. His partner being left holding the bag, so to speak, was so overwhelmed he died of a heart attack.

We did not know of these events until later, when I went back to Spain. It was then that I learned of my father's true motivation for our sudden departure. I also learned, in a grand stroke of karma, that when my father's ex-partner had died, another man took over the trucking business and became a millionaire!

Ruthless survival behavior seemed to run in our family and probably began long before my father, with his father my grandfather. Stories about my grandfather were part of the family mythology. Grandfather had been in the civil war in Spain, and fought against Franco. Franco was a dictator and Hitler's close friend. Grandfather had been captured by Franco's forces and placed in a concentration camp, in France according to my mother. I never knew which version of my family history was really true.

Here is where the story got interesting. The story was that grandfather had been shot at the camp and left for dead in a mass grave. As

As told to BARBARA RICH

with such hasty operations, the bodies were not closely monitored and Grandfather's wound did not kill him, even though he had been shot in the heart. The bullet had entered the heart and merely stayed there, for the remainder of his life. Digging himself out of the grave with his bare hands he had escaped to France. My father (his son) and mother became part of the household.

Grandfather was an unpleasant old tyrant and treated my mother as if she was merely a cook in his house. When I came along, he treated me (and everyone else) with contempt. Every interaction was a battle with him. I was a headstrong young girl and a finicky eater, which I am certain, drove my grandfather crazy.

I can remember one meal in particular. My mother had accidentally left an unpeeled whole bulb of garlic in a stew she'd made. I naturally could eat everything except the hardened cloves. Grandfather demanded that I finish everything on my plate. He locked me in his bedroom, in the dark, with this cooked garlic to eat. I stuck it under his pillow. The next day, I heard screams coming from his room. He had found the garlic. I'm not sure how I avoided punishment.

My mother was beautiful, but her looks more in keeping with the native peoples with a short, triangular face, slightly darker complexion and dark, sultry eyes. My parents met when my father was singing in a club.

If you compare two photographs of my mother, during a short ten-year span from this time to a decade later, her appearance alters greatly. In her earlier years, there is a sparkle to her smile and a glow that no doubt attracted my father to her. Later that glow seems to fade and my mother appears to age into a completely different person, tired and crushed under the burdens of her existence.

I am definitely a product of both of my parents with the stern temperament of my father, and a similar shaped face, hazel eyes, and the pleasant but common looks of my mother.

When we arrived in Colombia, I had never seen so many different shades of green and the dark reddish mud of the earth along with the brown skin of most of the natives, a warmth and comfort was created. When I close my eyes now and remember Colombia, it feels like I am being held in the loving arms of the Earth expressed through the color green.

We landed in Cartagena Oct. 12th. That was the anniversary of the day Columbus had discovered America. Upon disembarkation of the ship in Cartagena we didn't go directly to my Aunt Nena's house, as was the plan. We stayed in a hotel for a couple of days, while our freight from the ship had to be transported by bus to Pereira.

The first thing that caught my eye was the metal bars on the windows in our hotel. I didn't know if this was where we were going to stay while we visited family, so it frightened me. I recall some bits and pieces of those few days at that hotel in Cartagena. There were big wooden and leather trunks with our belongings, and the lack of a doll with no hair and no clothes that I thought had been packed. I found out that my parents had thrown it in the trash before we had left.

When I discovered this tragedy, I told my parents that we were going to have to return to Spain and get my doll. Of course that was out of the question.

To change the subject I was told that were going to meet "good family" on my mother's side, that there would be many cousins, aunts and uncles. This information made me feel better and I forgot about the hairless doll.

The two days I spent in Cartagena were strange and memorable, and probably had an impact on me in later life. When we landed, I had to go to the restroom. We were already off the ship and had yet to check into the hotel, so my father took me to a public restroom and stood outside the door like a sentry. I didn't know the danger at the time, but rape was a real possibility even for children. No one was truly safe there. Every kind of vice and corruption was blatantly encouraged.

The next morning we went to an open air, street market that seemed to be run by black people. My eyes were widened by the sight of these dark-skinned folks the likes of which I had never really noticed before, but I was completely shocked when I saw two of them having sex in the street behind one of the stands! I had also no real notion about what sex was at the time. So seeing these antics was a complete shock.

Colombian culture was new to me, so I looked to see my family's reaction to what I was seeing as if this might be common in this new country. It appeared that no one saw what I did. At least, they did not react. The woman was heavy-set. The man was swarthy. I knew their hair and skin were different. All of these people's teeth seemed so white in contrast to their dark skin. I remember thinking that Spaniards seemed more physically fit to me and I liked our fair skin, by comparison.

When our freight had been put onto a bus we prepared to take a propeller airplane from Cartagena to Bogota. My first experience on a propeller flight was frightening, partly because I overheard my parents talking to the pilot.

"There is severe rain in both Bogota and Pereira—our final destination. High altitude pilots in South America are some of the best in the world. They call the airstrip at Pereira, "The Hole," because the airfield is bordered on all sides by mountains and tall, rainforest trees. The dips between the huge Andes Mountains required an expert pilot to maneuver. And, because of the terrain, there was a lot of turbulence. We had to wait two hours before we could make the final leg of our journey.

PILAR

Even though we waited for the weather to clear, it was still raining when we arrived in Pereira. Wasn't that the whole reason why we'd waited? I heard them say, *"Pilots can't see the airport if it is raining. There is no room for error. We have to drop out of a high altitude, straight into, The Hole."*

Somehow everything was all right, even though it felt like an elevator sinking through the basement floor. That's how straight down our landing seemed, like a roller coaster hitting the bottom of a giant downhill.

When we finally arrived in Pereira, I had never seen the land before and was extremely impressed. Small round hills eventually gave way to high mountains and jagged peaks. The majestic Andes were shrouded in clouds and mist, rising in the distance. The only splashes of color were in the sky, which was cobalt and in the whites of the children's eyes that watched us pass. Occasionally there was a bright yellow adobe house. The color yellow was believed would deter mosquitoes. I never found this to be the case.

As told to BARBARA RICH

When we arrived at our final destination, there were about twenty people there to meet us, including my mother's sister, a woman who would become extremely important in my life. She and her husband, my uncle took me under their wings.

Her name was Leonor, but my mother called her Nena. Most everyone else referred to her as my crazy aunt. There was no love lost between these sisters. The rumor is that Nena was very flirtatious and wild. She and her husband, my uncle Oscar, were like my adoptive parents. They had a big impact in my life, because Uncle Oscar was the father I never really had. Uncle Oscar paid for my private school and helped to support my family for many years.

During that time I raised many an eyebrow at school with my wild behavior. My reputation at that Catholic school spread quickly. I can't tell you how many times the nuns hit me with a ruler, as they attempted to teach me some manners. I did not like the nuns. I felt like they were trying to break me and that I needed to retaliate to their every move.

I remember once I cut pictures out of Pedro's porn magazines and put a picture of a

PILAR

naked man under the nun's pillows! These women were much crazier than Nena ever was to me. When they discovered who was responsible for their pillow-pictures, the nuns sicked Dobermans on me!

Never one to surrender, I was so brazen I would retaliate each punishment with some new prank. Needless to say, my time spent at this school was memorable.

Nena had a wild streak in her. I am like her in a lot of ways. She took me aside on day, "Pilar, she smiled as she sat beside me, "You're growing into a very pretty young lady and your hormones are raging right now. I know you are going to have sex, but don't be stupid and ruin your life. I am going to give you birth control pills to protect you from becoming pregnant." I was only thirteen.

And thank God she did, because quite soon—or perhaps because I had the pill--I lost my virginity.

As Nena grew older she appeared very sexy, with big boobs accentuated by slutty outfits. Uncle Oscar let her do exactly as she liked. One of her pick-up lines involved a blood pressure band. She would carry this device around with her and ask to take the blood pressure of strange men she'd just met. No one seemed to care that she wasn't a nurse. And, while she took their blood pressure she would lean far forward to make sure they noticed her overflowing breasts. All her outfits were low cut and revealing. She was something, but I loved her and am grateful to her and Uncle Oscar for all they have done for us.

One of Nena's many friendships was with Jose, a Ping-Pong instructor. Her daughter, Christina and I became quite good at the game. We were playing in local tournaments and eventually were afforded the pleasure of traveling to Cartagena. We were so excited.

Being by the ocean again gave me a feeling of freedom. We traveled to many cities by the sea and won many tournaments. This was a perfect time in my life to be interested and enthusiastic about something other than drugs and substance abuse. I know it saved me from the web that snared my brother and sister into a life of addiction, because it let me see that there were other passions we could pursue in life.

Honestly, however I don't miss the competition. I may have only participated to get me out of the house. I may have been wild, but

PILAR

I wasn't stupid. My sister and I were both subjected to the double standards of a Hispanic household. We were forced to attend parochial school.

We stayed awhile with my mother's family until Papa could secure work. My father was very enterprising. He had many businesses and seemed to succeed at whatever he tried.

It wasn't long before we were moving into a large home with a backdrop of the Andes Mountains. We prospered in the town of Pereira for about a year, then financial woes forced us to move to a much smaller apartment: two small bedrooms, a kitchen and bath.

When we made the move, things were not so pleasant, I recall. Mom had become agitated and angry. She was always talking to friends or family members about my father. "He is seeing someone. I know it. I found receipts in his pocket for things he bought for her!" she whispered to *mi tia*. My aunt tried to comfort her, but she knew—in that way a woman always knows.

One day I was playing outside when a stranger approached our house. It was a woman who caught my attention because of the large amount of make up she was wearing.

The door of our apartment flew open and my mother came out to meet her in the street as if she knew her. Then, unexpectedly she merely stopped, stared for a moment at her and said,"Esperanza what are you doing here? This takes nerve, even for you. How could you do this to our family?"

"I'm not doing anything to your family. He's just as much my husband and the father of my children as he is yours."

My mother was shocked at the boldness of this woman's words, but showed no signs of disagreement. The next thing I saw was this woman's fist flying unprovoked into my mothers face!

Oh my God! I was as stunned as my mother should have been. *Why doesn't she hit her back?* But my mother just stood there, seemingly defenseless. The woman turned and vanished, as fast as my mother's face began to swell.

Soon after, but lasting weeks like the tail of a comet, the swollen face was followed by a lingering black eye. I was too young to fully understand what was going on at the time. I knew my father was *with other women*.

PILAR

However, I never really knew the full extent of his insulting behavior towards my mother.

It was the entirety of what my mother talked about. It also seemed to be the part of *his* character that everyone, including my mother accepted. I do not have a clear memory of how long it took for my mother to become this beaten woman. I was young and only remember her from about this time onward. What I do remember is that everyone did my father's bidding as if he was royalty.

When I was older I found out that while in Colombia, before I was born, my father had not only impregnated my mother, but also the housekeeper at the same time. When my mother realized what was going on, she was hurt and embarrassed.

At the time my family, Dad, Mom, Pedro and Carmen all took the ship back to Spain. I was the embryo my mother carried on this journey back. My mother was eight months pregnant. News traveled on to Spain that the housekeeper had birthed a son three weeks before I was born in Barcelona, Spain. Later I would be introduced to that very same boy, my half brother, when we returned to Colombia.

As told to BARBARA RICH

I am sure there are countless other children my father sired out of wedlock. When I think of it today, I am as stunned at the behavior of my father, but more that he got away with it.

Amid all this beauty, lurking in the shadows of the Andes was the dark side. Corruption was running rampant in Colombia, one of the largest drug cartels in the world. Any drug, or other vice was yours for the asking. Children were using and peddling all kinds of drugs at a very early age.

It was virtually impossible to escape this world-web of drugs. When you are dealing drugs you are in the company of vandalism, theft and murder. When you're hooked on drugs, you become its bitch.

"Who wants a cerveza?" I heard Pedro shout to his amigos. "Let's party, man."

Pedro didn't hear me as I peeked into his room (through the window in the bathroom). A bevy of naked men were strewn across the bed in his room.

"I'll have another, mi amor," came a voice from one of the guys on the bed.

PILAR

"Coming right up," he smiled as he stood there, his shirt opened down to his waist.

As I mentioned earlier, Pedro and I were very close and built a solid bond. Pedro's friends, gay or straight were more a family to me than my very own family. I felt loved and protected in their company.

I vividly remember, when we were younger, sitting at a large family dinner while we were in Spain. Everyone was talking and eating, enjoying the bounty of good food. There was always a dipping dish with wine and sugar. A loaf of bread would be cut lengthwise, slightly hollowed out and soaked with red wine. Pedro and I really loved dipping our bread in this mixture. This was common in our culture. To make it more appealing, the bread was then covered with sugar.

"*Donde esta Pedro, Mama*?" I wanted to know. "Where is Pedro?"

"He must have wondered off somewhere." Mama said calmly.

Before long everyone was searching for Pedro. Apparently Pedro dipped a little too much bread in the wine and got drunk! He wandered off all right and fell in a ditch. It was quite a sight to see, Pedro staggering as he tried to get his footing. Pedro and I laughed and laughed for days after. And still today we recall many fun times spent together. At times as I look back on my early childhood and smile with delight.

When we got to Colombia there were so many new temptations, it was inevitable that both Carmen and Pedro would get sucked into to the spiraling pit of substance abuse. Good fortune, or perhaps my young age spared me from the exact fate. But, let's not get ahead of ourselves.

The floodgate of these memories was opened on that kitchen floor that I would have to deal with at a later time in intensive therapy. From where I knelt at this moment, one particular scene was vividly replaying in my head.

"Carmen, Pilar go see your papa. Papa wants you to give him a foot massage."

The room was small. My dad lay on the bed inviting Carmen to come lay on the bed. I could hear the hum of the fan as I sat there watching. At first, he started caressing her, and very slowly started exploring private areas of my sister. She didn't move or speak; she just lay there, perhaps out of fear or familiarity.

I don't know how many times this may have occurred prior to this memory. He stroked her with one hand and began to unzip his pants with the other. I watched wide-eyed and curious, but also too fearful to move. He took his penis and began to penetrate her most private part.

"Is this what Papa did with other women, when my mother said he slept with them?" I wondered. *"Is Carmen being hurt?"* But oh, no, Mommy sent us in here. She would be very mad if Papa had hurt Carmen, wouldn't she?

There may have been many nights like these. I know that we were called upon to give many *massages*. Carmen never ever spoke of this. When it was over, it was over--till next time.

As I grew older I became aware of my father's uncontrolled attraction to women and visa versa. He stood tall, cut a lean and vibrant figure with vivid blue eyes and jet-black hair. He was a man who knew that he was strikingly good looking and had charm to match. I now saw my sister as a beautiful young woman with all the sensual attributes that would attract any man. This awareness did not change the horror of what I had witnessed. But, it was a horror that I did not fully understand when I first witnessed it.

As time went on I began to remember. Something must have happened, where I could not consciously go on living this nightmare. I neatly buried these episodes in the recesses of my mind.

"*Papa,*" I breathed, "*It was Papa!*" The words were torn out of me, out of the subconscious depths where they lay hidden all this time.

Beads of sweat started to form on my forehead as this startling revelation awakened in me. I had watched my father rape my sister! More rage surfaced, as I remembered my father abuse my sister, who had never spoken a word about it.

My face froze in horror! I gasped and fell to the floor, onto my knees and looked up from the sink. I suddenly realized the reason why I had concocted the story about my husband. The problems and the dangers of a philandering spouse and sexual addict didn't relate directly to my marriage, but went much deeper than I could have imagined.

Slowly I rose from the floor, still dazed, but as if a weight had been lifted. The truth was like a giant weight that I had been carrying my whole life. I had been trying to pretend didn't exist, even while I carried it.

Finally I understood my crazy thoughts and actions. All these years, suppressing these horrors in my childhood. How did I let this happen? How did Carmen, my mother and my brother allow this to continue? And, how did this relate to my current situation? Why was I only remembering it now?

"Pedro, I must call Pedro." I said out loud to myself, as I searched for the phone, my fingers fumbling for the numbers.

"Hola Pedro. It's Pilar. Do you remember when we lived in that small apartment in Colombia?"

"Yes," his answer was simple but seemed to have a certain amount of fear concealing a secret. "Why are you asking?"

"I just had a memory, or a vision of something terrible that I may have witnessed."

"Does it have anything to do with Papa?"

As told to BARBARA RICH

Pedro knew! But, how? "Did Carmen ever say anything to you about Papa? Did she mention anything about the so-called foot massages?" I asked, hoping he could shed some light on some of these faded memories.

"Carmen never told me anything about it, but I suspected. I do remember when we were on the ship going to Colombia he was molesting her."

I felt as if a brick had fallen on my head. How could Pedro have let this happen? What did he mean, *molesting her*? He was very vague, having apparently repressed some images of his own that he did not want to recollect. All in all, he had not known about the foot massages, but did know that our father was a sex criminal, and with our own sister! What else had happened, and with whom?

The most startling and heartbreaking realization for me was that I had not been as close to Pedro as I had believed. He had kept this knowledge about our father from me for many years and would probably not ever have voiced it, had I not asked him to tell me what he knew.

Our family was being very casual about a serious situation. Everything was being swept under the rug. Was there no accounting for this kind of behavior? I felt sick to my stomach. I just wanted to lie down for a while. If I could only fall asleep and then wake up and find out this was all just a dream. I lay down on the couch and closed my eyes, praying that sleep and sweet dreams would follow.

As told to BARBARA RICH

Chapter four
<u>New York</u> and Why I became an American

There she stood, that great lady welcoming me to New York--The Statue of Liberty. I was as inspired as anyone had ever been at seeing the great statue in the harbor for the first time. Those words about liberty and freedom had been created just for me! I felt reborn, no like I was being born for the very first time as I gazed upon her in the New York Harbor. A new start, a new life was ahead of me. Nothing that every happened before that moment, seemed real. At twenty-one with three hundred dollars to my name, I was embarking on the first solo adventure of my life.

When I think back on those years in Colombia I want to cringe. The events leading up to my leaving Pereira, Colombia would be better described as an escape.

After the Ping-Pong phase of my life was cut short by circumstance, I continued to party with my friends. My mother had decided that it was too much effort to keep me and my cousin involved in a sport that had few

PILAR

opportunities for advancement. I really did not care, as I was not driven to compete. It was merely something I happened to be good at, and the travel was fun, even if I only traveled within Colombia.

I had, in the meantime discovered my sexuality and had many boyfriends, all of whom I slept with. Night after night there was a party somewhere. Some nights I would leave the front door open so I could sneak out at midnight and party until the wee hours of the morning. It was risky leaving your door unlocked in that neighborhood, but I couldn't climb out of a window. The windows were all barred. They may have been barred to keep intruders out, but I felt like I was a prisoner and these iron slats were placed there to keep me in. I was wild and reckless, like a caged animal that had found the door to his prison left open. Over time I built quite a reputation and it was not a good one.

However, I never touched drugs. Self-poisoning was a habit that was enjoyed by my brother, Pedro and my sister, Carmen I thought, and everyone drank alcohol. That did not seem like a problem to me at the time.

Carmen had grown into a smart and beautiful woman and she held an executive job at a hotel. She was closer to my mother and preferred to stay close to home in spite of her drug use. Later her drug use would escalate. Pedro was always out with his gay buddies, partying. I was bitter and felt resentment. I just wanted to get away from my house, like most young teenagers. My mother always seemed unhappy and I was always escaping from someone or something.

Javier, my cousin on my mother's side visited one day. "Tia mia" he said, as he embraced my mother. "How is my favorite aunt, and where is everybody? Where are Pedro and Carmen?"

"Pedro is out and Carmen is working," She sighed.

I heard the two voices in conversation, so I entered the kitchen.

"Pilar, I hardly recognized you," Javier beamed when I entered. "You have blossomed into a chica linda."

He looked me over, up and down, front and back as if inspecting the merchandise.

Javier was short, no more than 5'6" tall, very strong for his size, and ten years older than

PILAR

I. Never had I given him much thought or considered him as anything more than one of my many cousins.

"I've come to invite you all to a family gathering in Manizales," he said as he sat on one of the kitchen chairs speaking to both my mother and me.

"Pilar, you should go," mother encouraged. "It will be good for you to be with your cousins. They haven't seen you in a long time."

I wanted to get out of the house and I thought this would please my mother. So, I threw a few things into a sack and off we went.

We got into the tiny truck that Javier owned and he started the engine. Javier and I rode awhile making small conversation. He seemed very interested in what had happened to Carmen, whether she was still using drugs and whether I had an interest. He seemed shy at first, which led me to be more outgoing. I started talking about how I felt and what I hoped for in the future and then something caught my attention. I noticed we had missed the turn to Manizales.

As told to BARBARA RICH

"Javier, you missed the turn. Where are we going?" I questioned.

We had been traveling on this very windy and narrow road for more than an hour. To arrive at my aunt's house, we should have taken a sharp turn at a T-intersection. Instead we remained on the curve that led toward Bogotá.

Javier just looked straight ahead, but appeared to be becoming angry and agitated. I started to get frightened and told him that if he did not stop the truck, I would jump out. It was then that he wound up his right arm, wrapping it around his body and struck me with the back of his fist in my face. It was a blow that he seemed to have practiced. It was so hard and so unexpected, that I cannot remember anything after the moment of impact.

I remember regaining consciousness several times during that ride, and felt extremely nauseated. It was not uncommon for someone to become sick on that road to Bogotá, but I had the added influence of a concussion that probably added to the effect. If I began to become too conscious, Javier would simply strike my face once again with the back of his fist. I must have started to vomit, inside the truck at one point, because I literally awoke on my face, outside the auto. He was shouting to me to hurry up and barf so that we could, "Get on with it."

At another point, I awoke with him on top of me, the seats had been pushed all the way down to make it easier for him to rape me. If I tried to resist, he hit me repeatedly on my head and stomach. After a while, I opted for consciousness and allowed the rapes to continue.

I was completely in shock. At one moment, he was my cousin a guy who I barely knew, but whom I might not recognize in a crowd. That's how little I really knew him. The next minute, he was a monster, a rapist and naturally I could only think, "What did I do to deserve this?" As I think back on the whole thing now, I realize that, that thought, that inferiority complex about how my past behavior was catching up to me, was what he had hoped would develop.

He started to talk about how I was going to help him and the motivations for his actions suddenly became frighteningly clear. "We have to get married," he demanded at last.

"It's the only way for me to get out of this stinking country."

The whole sordid, nightmarish plot began to unfold. He had come to my mother's house in search of Carmen. He knew that she was having problems with drugs. But, he'd come to my house in search of his salvation. I later found out that he'd gone to several other homes, of different women who he believed might be his ticket to freedom. You see, Carmen and I were both young women with duel citizenship. Although we had spent most of our lives in Colombia, we had never given up our Spanish passport or heritage.

At the time, it was very difficult to get a work visa coming from Colombia. In fact, they were just not available no matter which country was your ultimate destination. Javier was willing to do anything to get out of South America. I'm not sure where he was actually trying to end up, or for what reasons, but I had fallen into his plan merely by being home at the wrong time.

If some other woman, or Carmen had been available to Javier, he would have taken them instead. I was the unlucky one and my mother was an unwitting conspirator in my kidnapping. For that is what our family outing had become. During the ten-hour drive he outlined, "How it was going to be."

In his head, he was convinced that his only way out of the country was to marry a woman with a European citizenship. If he was married to a Spanish woman, for instance, he could get a work visa and passport that would allow him to travel to Spain. Depending upon the route he took, he could easily end up anywhere on the globe, even the United States.

It did not matter that we were cousins. Our last names were different (since he was on my mother's side) and we could get married and get our visas in the same building in Bogotá.

His plan did have some merit. I knew that I could probably leave Colombia whenever I wanted. I had just never had any motivation to accomplish anything other than partying, until that moment. Now, all I wanted to do was survive and be free of this nightmare.

I wondered what was going to happen to me once we arrived in Bogotá. I should have suspected that violence would play a part in the story. As soon as we got into the city, I was struck by another fierce blow and lost consciousness once again. When I awoke, I was in a bed, in what appeared to be an apartment that Javier had acquired for this madness.

The windows, as with most I was familiar with in Colombia, had bars on them with the added protection of black paper, to keep prying eyes away from what was going on inside. The door had several locks and the bed was on an outside wall, so if I pounded on it, no one could hear. There were also mattresses and boxes and other padding around, in an attempt, I believed to muffle sound. When I awoke, I realized the full meaning of my predicament. No one knew where we were. My mother believed that I was at my aunt's house in Manizales, so it would be days, perhaps weeks before anyone might become suspicious. Based upon my brutal treatment, the mental anguish and rape and seeing how prepared Javier was for this crime he was committing, I knew that I had to gain his confidence if I was going to survive. Obviously, if things did not work out with me here, Javier was going to have to kill me to make room for his next "fiancé to freedom."

I was a prisoner in that room for, what I determined was more than three days. Soon

PILAR

after arriving, I started the process of appearing to become Javier's ally. I told him that I understood his concern and realized that I could help him, if he'd let me. "You are going to have to trust me at some point," I said.

Javier knew something of human psychology and behavior. He used basic pleasure and pain to sway me to his position. He also was no mere fool, and I had to contend with his suspicion that I was saying and doing anything that I could to escape. I knew that my ticket to freedom was more difficult to obtain than simply getting past the locked doors and windows. I really had no idea where we were, but I knew that we were in Bogotá. I only knew the direction we were heading, when the beatings and rapes had started. And, if I was in Bogotá, that didn't mean that I only had to get away from him and justice would prevail. After all, I was in Colombia. Whatever I was going to accuse him of, in this ultra-macho-minded culture, would be questioned as the actions of a young woman who was a known party girl. The longer I was there, the less the bruises showed. No one would believe that I was in danger from my cousin, no less.

As told to BARBARA RICH

I had to get out and assess the situation, before making a clean escape.

"Let me prove myself to you, Javier," I said. "Let me show you that I want to help you."

The path to freedom began with consensual sex. He let me loose from my shackles long enough to clean my wounds and to use the restroom daily a few times a day. During one of these times, I did what I had to do to convince him that my running away was no longer a threat. In about four days, I was getting a little more relaxed and clear headed and I slept by his side like an obedient wife.

When he was convinced that I had succumbed to his brainwashing techniques, he took me out into the world for a short trip to the market, and allowed me to buy some toiletries and clothes. I made no attempt to escape or alert anyone to my situation. I laughed and joked and thanked him for being so generous when he paid for the few items I found. He seemed truly impressed with himself. His plan seemed to be working to perfection.

The next step was to go to the Government building and apply for a wedding license and a visa, in that order.

PILAR

"Why haven't you gotten married before this?" A stern-faced woman asked Javier.

"We were planning on marrying when we got to Spain, with the families, "Javier answered, having planned this for some time. "But, if we get married now, it will make the visa process easier."

And, it was true. Everyone in the office of immigration looked favorably on the wedding. They clearly stated that I would be able to get a visa easily, because of my Spanish citizenship, and that Javier would likely fair better marrying me first. The plan was coming together exactly as he'd hoped. The ceremony (a civil one) was set for the next day. I knew that the window for a safe escape was narrowing. I had to leave today.

When we drove back to the apartment, I gushed at how wonderful it was going to be when we got to Spain. I did not want Javier to suspect that there was any chance I was planning an escape.

"Don't you want to call your family before we go?" He was testing me.

"No, we can call them from Spain. I don't want anything to happen that might foul things up," I replied with a smile.

Somehow, he bought it. I had gained his confidence and he was getting sloppy in his arrogance. While we packed, I found his wallet unattended and took all the cash I could. He left the room for, what he said were "last minute business arrangements." When he did, I found some tools and removed the door from its hinges. I left the apartment and headed home. I found a taxicab and handed him about money I had stolen from Javier. He took me to the airport in Bogotá where I purchased my ticket with the rest; from there I took a flight to Pereira.

It was due to this strange turn of events with my cousin that made me leave Colombia and go to the United States. Pedro had arranged a place for me to stay for $70.00 a week in Queens. I got a job as a live-in nanny soon after and did that for a little over two and a half years. Originally, when I returned home after the ordeal with Javier, I had told Pedro of my plan to return to Spain, by way of New York.

PILAR

"If you can get a visa, I will pay for your ticket myself," he had said. He did not take into account my determination to leave Colombia. When I was being held captive, I had observed the corrupt system and realized that I was legitimately the best candidate for leaving South America. By continuing to honor my Spanish citizenship, I had given myself a foolproof method of departing, above most of the others that I'd met at Immigration. Routinely, I heard the word, "DENIED," uttered to man, woman and child. Woman with children in the U.S. were denied. Men with wives, mothers, or other relatives left behind were told no. Children, who had been separated from their parents or grandparents, were being kept from traveling, but I was different. I was a Spanish citizen. All I had to do was show my birth certificate, my Spanish passport and I was marched past all those who had been denied and straight to the visa department. My immigration back to Spain, via the United States was easily and smoothly approved while dozens of other desperate sojourners looked on in envy.

When I got home I told my brother, sister and mother what had happened. Pedro had gone to members of the family and made it clear that I was not to be bothered again. Javier apparently had gotten the message and decided it was not worth pursuing or worth starting a family war over. That was the way in Colombia. If you had a problem with one person, you did not deal justice merely to that one individual. You usually started off by torturing and killing a sibling, then climbed the ladder to child or spouse or parent, often making the person you had a problem with watch as all their loved ones perish, before taking your revenge on the original enemy. No one wanted that to occur in our family, so Javier simply vanished for a while and did not try to confront or stop me.

In about three months from the time of my abduction, I had gotten permission to leave the country. Luckily I had not become pregnant during my abduction. At that point, another clock started to tick. I had only three months to make all arrangements, including a round trip ticket to Spain via New York before the visa would be authorized. That's when I went to Pedro for help.

"You said you would help me if I got permission to immigrate. Well, I've got it. I have three months to leave, or I have to reapply."

"I said I would help and I will. When do you want to go?"

"Before the three months are up and as soon as possible."

"I think I can get the money together in about two months."

"I don't know how I will ever repay you."

"Don't worry, we'll think of something."

It was nearing three months when Pedro told me that he'd gotten the money he promised together and that he'd purchased a ticket to Spain, via the United States. I had no real intention of going to Spain, any time soon, but to secure the visa I had to purchase a flight ticket that would eventually return to my home country. What I really wanted, of course was to leave Colombia, at any cost. Being a Spanish citizen was my ace in the hole.

I will never forget that twelve-hour drive to the American Embassy in Bogotá. The old bus was like a broken down truck with chickens and unsavory peasants wearing ponchos and carrying machetes. These peasants were in the habit of drinking *Aguardiente*, an eighty proof liquor.

After my recent experience with Javier I was very frightened. Twelve hours in this company was brutal. Finally when I arrived, I scurried to the Embassy only to find it was closed! My heart sank with frustration and disappointment. It was the fourth of July, the day of American Independence.

What an irony! My bid for independence was being stymied by the most sacred holiday of a country that worshiped independence. I was not aware of this holiday being a citizen of Spain. Now, I needed to scrounge up what little money I could, to find a hotel for the night and return first thing the next day.

Finally I had my necessary papers. Another weight had been lifted. I could hardly wait to start my journey out of Colombia. First I had to get on that dreaded bus with more stinking chickens and machetes and return to Pereira.

There was a small gathering of friends and family to say goodbye and wish me well as I embarked on my next adventure. My mother did not try to stop me. Her opinion was that I had probably brought a lot of my problems upon myself, simply by the fact that I was a "wild child." But, she also knew that no one could ever reach his or her full potential in a country like Colombia.

Carmen had taken care of my initial lodging in New York by calling in a favor with a friend there. My brother knew it was crazy for me to stay in Colombia, because he knew what had happened with my cousin. In Colombia, stories of vengeance and payback were as commonplace as the daily newspaper. Pedro loved me and wanted to protect me.

My Aunt was the only one who expressed her disappointment. "Pilar," she said. "You've never worked a day in your life. What are you going to do?" Of course she was right and the question needed to be asked. But this heightened fever I had to break away, did not consider any new obstacles. I decided I would scrub toilets if I had to.

Other friends also thought that I was destined for failure. The only thing I'd ever done with any success had been Ping-Pong and helping around the house with my younger cousins. Pedro took this limited resume and made arrangements to smooth my landing in New York.

Once I got to New York, I looked in the Spanish paper for a nanny position. I went to an employment agency and in about a month they found me a position as a "live in" nanny. With the nanny job, the problem of my basic needs (food, shelter and a job) would all be taken care of with one solution. I was earning fair wages and meals were included. I had my big brother to thank for all that I had (my ticket for instance) and all that I was looking forward to. I would never forget the debt that I owed.

One of the first jobs I had as a nanny was with an Orthodox Jewish family. The father was a Rabbi. They lived in White Plains, which was outside of Queens, so I had to take the subway to work. Since I was raised a Christian, learning to adapt to the Jewish culture was difficult, especially with the language being another challenge. The Rabbi had Friday night rituals, with candle lighting and it seemed prayer was a constant theme.

Linda, another nanny who worked next door, and I became friends. We would take the children out for walks together and chat about different things. She spoke fluent English and

PILAR

was very helpful in improving my use of the language. One afternoon she invited me to lunch. She made the most delicious spaghetti and meatballs. There was so much I couldn't finish it all. Linda insisted I take it home and have it later.

Early the next morning I woke to screaming and yelling. "Pilar, Pilar what have you done? Where did you get these meatballs?" demanded the Rabbi.

I was stunned at first, still trying to get the sleep out of my eyes. I explained the best I could what had happened. Apparently there was pork in the meatballs!

The family proceeded to sanitize and purify their house. After that episode, I packed my things and left.

The winds of Fortune certainly shift quickly. Suddenly, I found myself with just fifty dollars in my pocket and no place to go, exactly what Pedro had tried to prevent.

I was standing on a street corner, thinking to myself, "Fifty dollars! What can I do with just fifty dollars?" Incredibly I was not depressed. I was almost elated. Here it was, another step on the grand adventure of life. I took a train to Grand Central Station and found a bench to sit on while I planned my next move. I had no place to sleep, so I had to spend the night in Grand Central Station.

People of every color and size were moving about at all hours, a loud speaker was blaring out some unintelligible information as my eyes searched aimlessly.

"Do I eat? Should I find a place to stay?" I sighed, while suddenly feeling alone and very vulnerable.

Then, just like an angel, a woman approached me. I must have appeared in need of some assistance because she moved through the bodies that were coming and going to specific places and headed straight for me, through the shadows and bad lighting of the station.

"What's your name?" She asked as soon as she was close enough.

"I am Pilar," I began, and proceeded to explain to her my tale of woe, as if her simple question was my cue to share a detailed story of my life. The words flooded out of my mouth as if it were a recorder that was being played by someone else. I could only, barely hear the words I was saying, which were few, but descriptive. Finally I stopped talking ad just looked at her with pleading eyes.

"My name is Juanita, perhaps I can help." She replied with a smile.

After a very short conversation this total stranger offered her home to me while I searched for work.

I had no alternative choices and took her up on her offer. To try and repay her incredible kindness, I cared for the house and did some babysitting for the month I spent there. Juanita's only condition for assisting me was that I looked for work in my spare time.

In those days I did not speak English well, and this was going to limit me in my search for employment. On my way to my first interview Juanita helped me write a note on the outside of a notebook, in English and Spanish, of the various information I would need to show at the train station and bus stops to arrive at my interview.

"Show this note to the people at the train station and each bus transition, Pilar," she instructed. "The conductors and drivers will direct you where to get on and get off."

The note read something like: *What is the name of the station in Yonkers for the train?*

As told to BARBARA RICH

What is the stop for Cireswoot? What bus should I take?

I could barely speak English, which made these job-hunting journeys quite a challenge, but I didn't care.

This new freedom I felt—and an apparent streak of dumb luck--drove me to meet every challenge as it was presented, with a confidence that I not only would survive, but also exceed even my expectations. My life seemed almost charmed.

I showed the note to an officer in Harlem. "Young lady," he warned, "Harlem is not a safe place for you to go." He quickly directed me out of there. When I think of it now, Harlem was a piece of cake compared to Colombia. But nevertheless, I was grateful for his advice.

When I got on the bus, the driver wouldn't take my money. I thought he was just being kind and I was being blessed once again. I was unable to understand that he needed the exact amount of the fare and could not make change. Eventually this confusion was resolved when another passenger offered me change and explained in broken Spanish what was going on.

PILAR

After this, I showed the driver the address I needed to get to for my interview. He was very helpful, using the map above his head to direct me, accompanied by hand signals. When I stepped out of the bus he told me to be careful. I did not get that job, or the next or the one after that, but in a few weeks I was moving forward once again. I got another nanny job and again my basic needs were being met.

Again, I was doing quite well. I had what I called my "dream job," no weekends, no buses or subways. It was ideal.

Gradually I had picked up quite a bit of English from the families that I was fortunate enough to work for, but I felt that I really needed to attend a school to learn more if I was ever going to truly succeed in America.

On my first day to the Adult School, I looked up the long flights of stairs that led to the classroom, feeling like I was back in Parochial school and about to face the nuns once again. I dragged myself up the stairs and through the doors. There were about twenty-five to thirty students from all different parts of the world. I felt immediately better and my whole attitude changed with one look at the instructor. I had that feeling you get when you see something you want. My heart started to flutter. *"This is the man I am going to marry."* I thought to myself. This was John Cameron, the man who would eventually become my husband.

I was drawn to everything about him. He was smart, funny and good-looking. I looked forward to Saturdays just to be near him. On that first day we covered many topics in a variety of ways. All the students seemed to be enjoying themselves and John made the learning fun. He was a big part of their enjoyment, as well. There was no big fanfare when I entered the room. He merely asked my name and suggested that I join the group by finding an empty seat.

"Thank you," I said in English.

"You are welcome," he responded and everyone nodded as if the simple exchange was a great beginning of my new appreciation for the English language.

Time flew by with repetitions and illustrations of different scenes. Eventually the instructor, John Cameron glanced at the clock on the wall. The round, schoolroom clock indicated that it was already 9.p.m. "Okay class, that's it for the evening. See you all next week."

The class of assorted foreigners rose, and there was the sound of rustling papers and shuffling feet as they collected their things and left the classroom.

I continued this routine throughout the classes. John showed me no more overt concern than any other student, but I knew he paid a special attention to me. After I successfully completed the course, *Mr. Cameron* wrote his telephone number on the blackboard in the event that someone might need to call him. I immediately jotted it down, not really believing that I would ever have the courage to call. That moment would never come however and I did not have to worry long. That last day he came up to me when we were all saying goodbye and asked, "Can I call you sometime? I'd like to take you out for dinner."

He smiled. He was so handsome I couldn't wait to say, "I'd like that very much." It was the first conversation that we'd had, that was not part of an English lesson. It felt very natural. He called me that very night. In spite of my surprise and delight, I just knew it would happen.

We started dating regularly and John opened up a whole new view of New York for me. We went to movies and plays and sporting events. It wasn't that he was trying to find something that we were both interested in. It was more that we loved to do just about anything, as long as we were together.

As if we had been together for years, I was spending the night at his place one evening and he woke me up. "Pilar, marry me," he said with conviction. I looked up at him trying to get the sleep out of my eyes. I thought I might be dreaming.

"Are you sure, John?" I asked, now sitting up and looking at him.

"Yes, I'm sure," he answered as he tenderly placed a kiss on my lips.

Now I was wide-awake. "John, I just want to make this clear. I don't iron and I want to continue working. On November 6th in a civil ceremony at city hall we were married after just four months of *courtship.*

We still had stardust in our eyes for the first years of marriage and my charmed life seemed even more magical with John in it. It was a good time for us. John had been working as a teacher part-time because he'd lost his original job on Wall Street. After we got married, he took a job with the Rockefeller family and I was making decent money as a nanny. Our savings grew. We were saving our money so we could move to California, where he was born.

John had family there and we both loved the ocean. After about five months, we left New York and headed for Southern California. John's grandparents had a place in Laguna Hills. We stayed with them awhile.

I didn't have to complete the citizenship paperwork, because, while I had started the process when I was hired as a nanny, now that I was married to an American citizen I got a Green Card in about two weeks. It was temporary, only because it took a little time to receive the permanent residency status. In those days, it took seven years from the time of legal residency until I was able to claim citizen. Now, however, I am an American.

In fact, now I still have my Spanish citizenship as well as Colombian. Perhaps I should have become a member of the U.N.!

My first job in California was as a preschool teacher. I had experience with children because of my years of being a Nanny.

As told to BARBARA RICH

I got the job with ease. Then, when we longed for improvement, I started looking for something else. One of the parents of the children I was working with told me that she knew of a job as a bank teller. I decided to apply.

I knew I was good with numbers, so a bank teller seemed like a good choice for a job. I interviewed for this part-time job and got it. They ended up hiring me full-time!

Now, being truly bilingual didn't hurt. My new employers could not believe that I hadn't studied English for many years, and had been in the U.S. such a short time. I believe that the preschool children are very much responsible for teaching me English.

I also applied at a major cell phone company for a position in the billing department. Things were working out nicely. John had gotten his masters degree and was now working for a financial firm. We would be able to afford a place of our own.

Finally we got a place in San Clemente. I was able to quit one of my jobs at Bank of America and pursue my other job with the major cell phone company. Cell phones were at their height of sales and I could advance there.

PILAR

After about three years John went back to school. Our focus was on our careers and we prospered. It wasn't until eight years later that we decided to start a family.

This was one of the more stable and happy times of my life. It seems I had fought so hard to get to where I was loved and respected.

About three years after moving to San Clemente, we heard news from Colombia. "Oh my God, Pilar, Pedro is in jail. What are we going to do?" my sister said. I could hear the panic in her voice.

"What?" I asked in shock. "Calm down and tell me what happened."

I could hear her take a deep breath. "He was on his way to Spain and he was caught with the drugs that he was delivering"

"Pedro, Pedro, Pedro," I thought to myself. "How could you be so foolish?" but I said, "Carmen, don't worry. Let me make some calls and I will get back to you"

"I'm really scared Pilar, what if..."

I interrupted her and repeated that I would look into it and get back to her. After I hung up the phone I felt like I was just punched in the gut. I tried not to get hysterical.

"My family, always my family," I screamed inside my head. The family ties held me bound from the freedom and respect I strived for. I cried for a long time before I started making calls.

"How can I repay you Pedro, you have done so much for me?"

"Don't worry I'll think of something." These were the words that came rushing into my mind as I remembered when I thanked Pedro for his help getting me to America.

Of course, I would have to do something to help. I couldn't forget that if it hadn't been for Pedro I wouldn't even be here in America. John and I discussed at length what we should do.

"Pilar," John said, feeling my concern. "We just do not have enough money to afford an attorney, especially one that is working on the other side of the Atlantic."

"We both know," I replied, by way of resigning myself to John's logic. "A public defender is not going to even try and get an acquittal."

"Probably not. So, I think you and Pedro might have to start facing the possibility of jail time." Pedro would have to get a public defender.

"But John, isn't there something we can do?" I pleaded.

"Pilar, I will think of something," John answered reassuringly. "I have a friend, named Paco in Madrid who possibly could help."

We made several calls trying to get advice and/or help to aid Pedro. For the time being Pedro would suffer the consequences of his decision to be a mule for drugs.

John, knowing how desperate I was to do something to rescue my brother, opened an account to begin saving for my trip to Spain. About nine months later we had saved enough for one ticket to Madrid.

John called his friend, Paco one more time and asked if he could offer further assistance. "Pilar is more than welcome to stay at my house while in Madrid, John. I'm happy to help. I will take her to see Pedro in Prison," Paco said sincerely.

"Muchas gracias, Paco. You are a true amigo." John said, relief showing like bright colors on his face.

John and I had visited Spain a few years after we moved to San Clemente, that's when I met

As told to BARBARA RICH

Paco and his lady-friend, Maria. We stayed with Paco at that time, so I felt comfortable staying there again. We also visited my aunt, my father's sister in Barcelona and caught up on the news about the project my father had left before we ran off to Colombia. What an extraordinary feeling I had after being away so long from my homeland. It had been years. My early childhood was spent here till I was seven years old. I can't put into words how I felt at that moment. So many fond thoughts found a path and I was transported there again. It was a lovely visit.

So, again I would return to my roots.

I had always kept in contact with my family in Colombia and they were relieved to hear I was going to Madrid to see Pedro.

Paco met me at the airport. I recognized him right away. He hadn't changed in the past few years.

"Mucho gusto Pilar. Bienevenida", he said as we embraced and gave a kiss on each cheek, a Spanish greeting. We exchanged social amenities as we walked toward the baggage area.

Paco shared his apartment with his girlfriend, Maria. It was a very nice three-bedroom house, with plenty of room for me to stay comfortably for a short time.

    I was thinking of the things I might need to bring to Pedro, clothes, books, etc. I was filled with anxiety, not knowing what to expect. Feeling anxiety and then actively ignoring it had become commonplace for me. At times I was momentarily so overwhelmed that I found myself just staring into space, trying to make my mind a blank.

As told to BARBARA RICH

Chapter five
Pedro's boyfriend

The prison was in a suburb outside of Madrid. The physical structure was nothing like I had expected. It was more like a resort compared to the prisons I had seen in Colombia. My brother had been caught carrying cocaine from Colombia to Spain, but was lucky to have been confronted on the Spanish side of the flight, rather than the Colombian.

Even though I was relieved to see the atmosphere was not very threatening, my first meeting with Pedro was a nervous experience. I did not know what to expect, and of course, as usual everything hinged on having the right paperwork. Luckily, I had gotten all the right permissions to visit my brother and the language was a familiar one.

On my first visit I was led to a brightly lit room with several chairs facing many windows along one wall. You could see through the windows that there was another room on the other side, with a row of chairs

PILAR

facing back. The glass went all the way to the ceiling and there as a counter and telephones on both sides for each person, visitor and convict to use.

Visitors were led into the room and directed to empty seats. There were small petitions between our seats, offering a small amount of privacy. We could see, through the glass a heavy metal door with a guard allowing inmates to enter, one at a time. They also were led to various seats to face their visitors on the other side. There was no physical contact this first visit. When Pedro was led into his side of the meeting area, he spotted me immediately. There was a big smile on his face and I knew he was happy to see me.

"Hello little sister," he said and placed his hand up to the glass.

"Are you ok?" I asked, tears welling up in my eyes.

"Don't worry about me," he said and after a few minutes of conversation, I realized that there really was no reason to worry. I knew there would be remorse, but I was surprised to hear that he took full responsibility for his actions. "I deserve to be in prison," he said.

"It's probably the best thing that could have happened. At least now, I'm clean."

I remember it was winter, so it was freezing outside and very cold in the meeting room. If it weren't for the bright lights, it may have been even colder inside. As it was, the lights gave off some heat. I supposed they did not want us to get too comfortable. Pedro asked about John and our mother and I told him what I could, though I really had very little information. Notably, he did not mention Carmen.

"What happened? Why did you do it?" I had a chance to ask, at last.

"I think I was set up," he said simply.

"Set up? Who would set you up?" For all my street smarts, and life experiences, I had made it a point not to learn too much about the drug-supported underworld in Colombia. I had seen what it was doing to my siblings and how an entire government seemed to function in complete response to the sway cocaine seemed to hold on the total populace. I knew also that one of the many, negative side effects of cocaine and crack use was paranoia. I had not seen this in Pedro, and after a few minutes of explanation, I was not sure if this was the case here.

"I was stopped going through customs at the airport in Spain," he said. It was as if someone knew that I was carrying drugs, knew about the drugs even before I had deplaned. I just don't know why."

There were several possibilities that ran through my mind. Pedro had been hanging around with a lot of bad people and I'm sure he was getting deeper and deeper into debt. You never knew, in Colombia who might be your enemy, and there were always the obvious enemies, such as my cousin the rapist.

"Well," he said at last. "At least it was better than being caught in Colombia." Ironically, with all the cocaine that passes through the county, some with government officials looking the other way, the sentences are much more severe.

"I could have gotten death!"

He went on to tell me that he had been treated very civilly at the Spanish airport. "They took me to a little room and looked through my luggage as if they knew what they would find. They did not waste time in any pockets, but unwrapped a shirt that had what they wanted. When they found it, they took me to jail. Nobody ever got excited and just before I was taken out of the examination room, they made a call to someone saying simply, '*We stopped him.*' I don't know who they were talking to, but that's what it sounded like."

The next day I felt better having seen Pedro and seeing how well he looked. Again I dressed very carefully because I wanted to project an image that would be respected by the Spanish gentlemen that were the guards. My tactic had a much better result that I expected. When I arrived at the prison, I was led to a more private visitor's room with locked door, two chairs and guard outside the door. The heat seemed to have been turned on, as I had to remove my coat to be comfortable. I waited only a few minutes when the door opened and Pedro was allowed to enter the same room that I was in. When we saw one another without the window he rushed to me. We embraced and both of us began to cry.

After a few minutes I took a step back and looked at my brother. I was surprised to see Pedro looked even better than the day before. As a matter of fact, he looked better than I had ever seen him when we were living in

Colombia. With all the negatives that there were about the situation, at least there were no drugs and that had been the one obstacle that my brother was unable to overcome on his own. When he was arrested, even before he had been convicted, Pedro was forced to clean up and he knew that if he had not been, it was only a matter of time until he was killed, directly or indirectly by the drug culture.

I'm sure that the idea occurred to him that he was paying fair price for his own addictive behavior. To this day however, I really don't know how many times he had smuggled drugs. He said this was the first time, which may be true. He may have been a lot of things, but Pedro was not a good criminal, so I tended to believe him.

He had been caught red-handed and given a maximum sentence of twelve years. Twelve years, is still, we assumed less than "life in prison." Later, when he came out of prison he was a changed man. He also did not suffer much while he was there except that he was away from his boyfriend and family.

Pedro had taken his entrepreneurial talents from the streets and made a comfortable place for himself in prison. He told me that he saved all of the spare fruit that he could from his meals in the mess hall and smuggled them back to his cell, stuffed in his pants. This fruit was then crushed and mixed together in large garbage bags that he stole from the cleaning carts in the hallways. To this mixture he added water and then carried around, close to his body until the fruit fermented. The prisoners (and some guards, I suppose) called the concoction "pruno," though any fruit with juice and high sugar content would turn to alcohol once it was allowed to brew.

Pedro told me later that the bags could be laid flat under the bunks so that it was easily concealed. Apparently, more than one bag fit easily under a single bunk, and Pedro became the prison bartender, in a sense. He had earned a certain amount of freedom from scrutiny, partly because of my visits. When I came to see him, I was always very polite and well mannered, which I am sure, served to his advantage. Everyone knew that I was his sister. They seemed to respect me, and by transference assumed that Pedro must have come from the same *good* stock.

"Pedro I will keep in touch and see how things are going. We will work something out."

PILAR

We embraced and that was the last time I saw Pedro until his release. I could rest easier knowing that his stay in jail was not by any means hard time. He also did not have to serve the entire twelve years. After four years, because of good behavior he was released, having paid his debt to society.

While he was away, however Carmen had entangled all of our lives into a very complicated mess. Apparently, Pedro had gotten word from one of his friends in Colombia while in prison about her and Carlos' (Pedro's boyfriend) activities. What he'd learned was the reason he did not mention her, or Carlos on my first or second visit together in prison.

My sister was no different from many other beautiful, young women. She may have known she was beautiful, but it was never enough. She always wanted more it seemed. She never was able to live up to her own standard. Low self-esteem and drug use often go hand in hand, as do being a rape victim and other self-destructive behaviors.

Maybe Carmen was trying to forget what my father had done to her. Being abused as a child also goes hand-in-hand with low self-esteem. Sometimes we set our standards and goals very low, because those low standards are the only ones we believe we can achieve. Maybe that was why she seemed to look for a man who would treat her as an object. I don't know. All I do know is that Carmen's use of drugs, and her low self-esteem caused her to make many more poor decisions.

Drug addicts often talk about the wreckage of their lives. The first wreck that Carmen was responsible for was a brief marriage that resulted in a pregnancy. The child was born in a period when drugs had not totally eclipsed her rational thinking. Carmen was twenty-one but I was only eighteen and observed from a distance what was happening with my siblings. For some reason I had placed myself slightly on the outside, like an observer of Pedro and Carmen's downward spiral. That's the way I am seeing things now. If I have to look back on my relationship with my siblings, I can almost observe myself, looking in through a window on their seemingly endless partying. I am not trying to make an excuse for not saving them. I know that we are all responsible for our own lives, not anyone else's.

PILAR

I am merely recounting the events as I see them, but also as I lived them. I lived as an observer, but I was also *in the picture being viewed*. It would have been like trying to change the actions of characters that we see on a movie screen. We may at times call out to them or gasp as they walk innocently into a darkened room, where we (the viewer) know that a killer or other monster is waiting. We can call out, or scream, but it will do no good. The movie we are watching has already been written, performed and filmed. If we don't like the outcome for the characters, we can only live our own lives, having learned a lesson from their misfortunes. Or, I suppose we can write another script, a sequel where we are the stars and we overcome the monsters.

Carmen's husband was of no real consequence. He could have been anyone who paid attention to a young woman who did not believe in herself. I will not dwell on him here. The pregnancy came fast, and was not unexpected. I don't know if she still had a shred of social dignity at that time, and married *because* she was pregnant or just made a bad mistake for some other reason and the pregnancy was the effect. The result was that she gave birth to a little girl, Carolina.

At first, Carolina was a distraction for her and the whole family. We loved mothering her and playing with her, but as time passed Carmen became more and more involved in the drug scene.

She had been spending a lot of time with Pedro and his friends and especially Pedro's lover Carlos. Like many young, and old people in Colombia, they all shared the same addiction to testing life and challenging death. The more they partied, the more drug use became a part of the scenario. Using drugs, and especially cocaine is engrained in the culture of Colombia.

This didn't just happen when my family arrived. It has been going on for thousands of years. The coca plant is really revered in the region. True, most of this is a cover for the sad fact that, as usual a few rich people exploit everyone beneath them in economic status, but there is a strange kind of pride that Colombians seem to have about being the cocaine capital of the world.

The Drug Lords rule the country like tribal leaders of ancient times, and the government is often openly in the service of these false-feudal leaders. If a government official gets a conscience and tries to stop a shipment or make an arrest, they are swiftly assassinated or just disappear. New puppets are put into their places and business as usual can continue.

The farmers are also an integral part of the system and are probably the most exploited. They make only slightly more money putting their lives and the lives of their families on the line, than they would by raising a less productive crop, but it is more.

So, while Pedro was away in prison, Carmen and Carlos had become lovers. Carlos was easily tempted by the charms and beauty of our sister, but he was also a classic manipulator. He had no job, no prospects and was leaching off of Pedro before my brother had gone away.

Carmen became pregnant with Carlos' child shortly after Pedro's conviction. It was fortunate for Carmen and Carlos that Pedro was serving time so far away and that he had years to cool off before encountering his old boyfriend and sister again.

As told to BARBARA RICH

The web of deception just got more and more tangled with each new twist in the thread of events. I learned about my sister's "situation" just before leaving for Spain, and had assumed that Pedro knew all about what she and Carlos had done in his absence.

The flight home was much calmer now that I had seen and spoken with Pedro. I almost felt relieved he was in prison. I knew he was clean and not suffering. My thoughts found their way to Carmen and her life in Colombia. "*Pilar,*" I thought to myself. "*You can't save everyone.*" I leaned back and closed my eyes. I was happy to be returning to John and my home, my safe haven. I fell asleep, lulled to slumber by the droning jet engines.

"Ladies and gentlemen please be sure your seatbelt it fastened and your seat is in the upright position. The pilot is starting our descent into Los Angeles." I awoke to the flight attendant's announcement over the speaker.

I was so happy to see John and feel the beautiful warm weather, after the freezing cold in Madrid. Soon I settled back into my regular routine at home, but periodically kept in touch with Pedro and the other members of my family.

PILAR

Slightly over a year had passed since Pedro had been arrested and I received a call from Carmen. "Pilar, it's a boy!" I heard my sister say.

How are you feeling?" I asked.

"Not that great," she answered.

During Carmen's pregnancy she was under nourished and using drugs. Because of her drug use, she needed money. In one of my conversations with him, she asked me for some money.

I later found out that Carlos, the father of the baby forged my sister's signature and took her I.D. card. He then cashed the check for himself. Just one of the many abusive and selfish acts he did during their relationship.

Her labor was horrible. It lasted for fourteen hours. Her situation was worsened due to her fragile condition. Her baby, David was very blue and needed oxygen because of many hours of labor. Needless to say I sent her the money she needed.

About two years later, I called Carmen and told her we were coming to visit. She was so happy to hear of our visit.

I discussed the trip to Colombia with John and he thought it might be nice to visit the family for a week or so. Colombia did not hold fond memories for me. But, this would be different. I would be with John and together we would be going to welcome a new member to the family. I thought of Pedro and how upset he was when he received the letter telling him, his lover, Carlos had gotten his sister pregnant!

We were lucky we were able to get away for this trip, without putting our jobs in jeopardy. Excitement mixed with anxiety rushed through my head, as I started packing and preparing for our trip.

Arriving in Colombia brought back so many memories. The smell of the streets, the impressive views of the Andes Mountains, the very culture of this country came flooding into my mind. I was wondering what we would find when we arrived in Pereira.

To say that I was disappointed upon our arrival, would be putting it mildly. Carmen looked terrible. Her appearance was disheveled and careless. She was not the well-groomed Carmen I remembered. My eyes wandered through this house that had been my home for so many years. I realized how fortunate that fate, even though I suffered to get there, had

PILAR

placed me in America, or anywhere else but Colombia for that matter.

My mother was the same, slightly absent woman that I remembered. We embraced, but not much was said. After dinner John and I were very tired after our long trip. I barely remembered that we used to sleep on beds of packed hay when I was growing up and the mattress in my old room was the same as it had always been. John and I endured the lumpy beds of hay for the length of our stay, but it was completely uncomfortable for both of us.

During our stay, Carmen and I had a chance to get away by ourselves one day and we talked about Pedro for the first time. She told me how difficult it was raising both Carolina and David. "Carmen," I asked. "Why Carlos? You knew he was with Pedro."

"Oh, Pilar, I feel very bad. I really do. We were both on drugs and lonely. It just happened," she explained.

"Pedro was so angry and hurt," I said. "It is a good thing he isn't here, but he will get out eventually. What are you going to do?"

"I don't know," she said. "I have not tried to contact him, because I was told that he doesn't want to talk to me at all right now."

We returned to our family home and did not talk about the situation again. Why worry about something that was not going to happen for many more years?

After observing Carlos for a few days, my opinion of him went from bad to worse. He was a total user who had it made. He was living in Pedro's house for free and stealing from my mother! Unfortunately, my mother feared that Carmen and Carlos would leave if she said anything and she did not want to be left alone, without her grandchildren. She would rather Carlos steal from her than face that terror.

Also, taking care of her grandchildren was the first positive thing that had happened to her in a long time. My father had been driven away when I was still very young, and we were all she had left.

My mother and I had never spoken about the abuse she had been a party to, and I did not know about it at the time when Carmen was living with Carlos in her house, but we never really had much in the way of direct communication between us.

I can only imagine that her ability to ignore the worst in people had come in handy when dealing with Carlos, just as it had when she had to endure living with my father. I guess, in a way Carlos might have been an improvement, only in so much as it was not her own husband who was having sex with her daughter. That Carlos was formerly her gay son's lover was one of those "little details" that she had, through practice, been able to conveniently ignore.

Looking back, my mother was the perfect personality for enabling this kind of horrible behavior. My God! She was able to ignore a punch to the face! The tangled perversity that was her family must have been relatively easy to accept.

So, Carlos leeched his way into a relationship, a family and home life (such as they were) without making any more waves. He was like a cockroach that thrives because the house where he lives is also infested with rats. Instinctively, I wanted Carlos out of their lives. He was a bad influence, among other things, but he was also a physical threat to my mother.

Most bullies are really no threat, but my mother was so frail and Carlos was stronger and prone to blustery outbursts. I thought he might hurt someone accidentally, while trying to throw his weight around.

As told to BARBARA RICH

While John and I were there, John tried to include Carlos into the family affairs. We decided to take everyone out for dinner, which was scheduled to take place directly after the christening of the newborn David. It was a typical Catholic christening, with all the pomp and circumstance that is customary in the South American countries. Since John and I were the godparents, it seemed like the "right" thing to do. This act of kindness seemed to irritate Carlos for some reason, and brought out an irrational jealousy for my lifestyle John and I were leading. At the end of dinner, we were about to leave, but had not finished every scrap of food on our plates.

"So I guess you both feel pretty proud of yourselves to be able to pay for this big expensive dinner for everyone," Carlos blurted out, after remaining angry and quiet for most of the dinner.

"I don't know what you mean," John said, trying to divert the conversation. "We are just happy for your new son and want to be good godparents."

"There are many people here in Colombia, even in your own family who don't have a fraction of what you two feel nothing about throwing away," Carlos added pointedly.

"If it makes you uncomfortable," John said quickly. "We can go to dinner without you from now on."

Carlos did not respond. Everyone realized that he was never going to be able to change his perception of what his life *could* be. He would always be a conman, sizing up his next con. He would never be a true father to David, or a partner to Carmen.

John and I were glad that we made the trip, if for no other reason than to observe what was happening in my family's household. We were also, relieved to be going home to our soft beds and familiar lifestyle.

"Pilar, I have a release date. I am getting out of prison in two weeks!" Pedro exclaimed. I could picture his excitement as heard his voice.

"That's good news Pedro. I can't wait to see you!' I was overjoyed with the news.

Pedro and I had discussed in earlier conversations that going to Colombia would be a big mistake given what had happened there. I knew he had anxieties about Carlos and Carmen, but even he knew it was too risky to return to Colombia. The only job Pedro could get in Colombia without training would be driving a taxi.

Driving a taxi in Colombia was pure suicide. Cab drivers were constantly being robbed or murdered. So his choices were to be a cab driver or back to drugs. The obvious choice was America.

I made arrangements for Pedro to fly to California and stay with us until he could get settled. At first everything was fine, but Pedro had difficulty with the language and consequently finding work was a real challenge. He tried, but he just was not comfortable in this country. He was like a fish out of water. Besides that, all the while he was with us the nagging thought of Carmen and Carlos together in Colombia was eating at him.

"Pilar, I'm sorry but living here is just not working for me." He sighed. "I need to get back to Colombia. I must get my house in order. I need to see Carlos and Carmen face to face."

"Alright Pedro, I think I understand." I walked over to him and looked straight into his eyes. "Pedro, promise me you will not get involved in drugs."

PILAR

"Don't worry, Pilar, I have learned my lesson. I am very aware of the dangers lurking in Colombia."

Well, I was definitely fulfilling my debt to Pedro. Again, I paid for a ticket for him to return to Colombia.

For a while Pedro stayed with some friends before going directly to his house. He didn't have any options as far as work was concerned, because of his age and recent prison stay. The only job he could get was the most dreaded job, that of a cab driver.

You might say he flirted with death every time he sat in that cab. I guess he was lucky.

Eventually he did go to his house to face Carmen and Carlos. What he found was a mess.

"I can't believe it," he whispered at first, but he could feel his own rage written on his face. " How could you? My own sister and my lover having an affair while I rot in prison!"

"Lo siento, Pedro." Carmen was crying now. "I never thought it would go this far, and then I got pregnant. Oh Pedro I'm so sorry."

"And you Carlos," Pedro turned to look at his ex-lover. "You're not only a cheat, but a thief and a con-man. Get out of my house," He screamed fire raging in his eyes. " I want you out! Do you hear me? Out!"

Carlos knew when he was defeated. He left, probably thinking where he would find the next sucker to support him.

Pedro had his work cut out for him. He practically had to redo his entire house to restore it to its original condition. Carmen was another story. Pedro tried on many occasions to tell her what a dangerous spiral her life was taking.

Shortly after Pedro left, I became pregnant with our first child. John and I had waited eight years and were looking forward to having a baby. Little Gabriela was born.

We just adored her. It was the first time I felt I had someone I could love so completely. The innocence of a child that I was free to guide and protect without the intervention from family or other outside influence. About a year and a half later we welcomed another beautiful daughter, who we named Sofia. They became the main focus of our existence. Our lives seemed so complete.

"I got an offer to go the Canary Islands (off the coast of Spain) and work as a chauffeur," he told me. I could hear the excitement in his voice. I was just glad to hear he was getting out of Colombia.

"Pedro, that is great! I cheered. "Tell me all about it."

Some friend of his had called him and told him about the position. He would be working at a beautiful resort. It sounded like a dream job for Pedro and just what he needed.

I knew he felt embarrassed to ask me once again to get a ticket for him to get this job.

"Pedro do you need money to get a ticket to the Canary Islands?" I asked

"Pilar, this will be the last time I will need help. I think this is what I have been waiting for."

"Pedro, John and I will pay for your ticket. I hope this is what you have been waiting for. I wish you the best of luck on your new venture "Buena Suerte!"

"Pilar, mi querida hermana, tu has hecho mucho por mi. Como puedo agradecerte," he said, thanking me for all I had done for him. "I am indebted to both you and John. John has been like the brother I never had."

As told to BARBARA RICH

"Pedro, if you can stay away from drugs and have a good life, that would be payment enough" I said, hoping he could make a clean slate for himself.

When John came home, we all went out to dinner and celebrated the good news.

After about a year, Pedro called and told us he had another offer from Lucia, a family friend of ours in Barcelona.

"This will be a great opportunity for me, Pilar," he said. "I will be doing something that comes naturally to me." I will be bartending and waiting tables in a beautiful restaurant and also be in our home town in Barcelona"

"It's sounds like a great opportunity, if that's what you really want Pedro. You know I only want what is best for you."

PILAR

As told to BARBARA RICH

Chapter six
All About John

"Let's go back to the reason that you originally came to me for help," my therapist was trying to rein me back to the starting point of my sessions. I was feeling as if things had gotten out of control in my life. What she was trying to show me, I think, was that I had never really had as much control as I'd wanted, or believed.

"Which was?" I was so caught up in all the new revelations, that I'd completely forgotten why I'd come to see her in the first place.

"You were having problems in your marriage."

"Oh, yeah."

"I want you to try and remember what you were feeling at that time. What led to your suspicions about John? Why did you feel that he was drifting away from you?"

I looked back in my mind and remembered that there was a time when John had been a rock for me. Without his support I would never have been able to help Pedro or my sister or mother to leave Colombia. What had gone wrong? Was it me, or him, or both of us, as the therapist was contending?

It was practically impossible to separate the recent infidelity with my uneasy feelings of so long ago. Perhaps, as the therapist pointed out there was no reason to separate them entirely. At first, I was not sure what was wrong. I begged John to see a therapist with me and he always seemed to have an excuse why he could not. Eventually I went on my own and discussed my feelings of depression and low self-esteem that I believed was completely due to my husband's dissatisfaction with me.

In a short time, my sessions turned away from our marriage and focused completely on my poor image of myself.

My suspicions that John was no longer committed to our marriage, as he once had been began as a feeling of uneasiness, like being slightly sick to my stomach. I felt that I was the cause of the illness as well as the one who was feeling sick. It did not occur to me that John was doing anything wrong. After all, in my experience of what a marriage was—my immediate family growing up gave me no healthy role models—John was beyond anything I'd ever seen. He was a great and committed father and had always supported me when I took on the added responsibilities of helping my siblings or my mother. He never failed me on an ethical level. It was only his moral and physical commitments that were suspect. I will be eternally grateful to John for his generosity and kindness toward my family, but the fact was that I was unhappy and John was no longer committed to the marriage. These two items alone might have been enough to predict disaster. Initially, however I had not known of his affairs and I had not yet remembered my childhood traumas.

What had gone wrong? When did I start to notice a change in John? What were the signs? It is a story in which many women have played a part over the years, but it always comes as a shock when a spouse is being unfaithful. In hindsight each woman looks back and says something to the effect, "I should have realized when..."

I probably should have realized that John had something else going on when he lost interest in sex.

PILAR

"How do you know he was not interested?" My therapist wanted to know.

"He started making excuses."

"Like he was too tired?"

"Sometimes. Or, he said that he was working on a case or his mind was preoccupied or that work was getting to him or that he just wasn't feeling well."

"What did you think was happening?"

"I thought somehow that it must be me. Maybe I was not attractive to John anymore. I wasn't thinking it through really. I didn't suspect that he was having sex elsewhere. That never occurred to me. I just knew that I wasn't having sex.

"How long did this go on before you realized there was a problem?"

"About a month."

As told to BARBARA RICH

Chapter seven
U.S.A: Spring 1999/Summer 2000

"Mama how was your flight?" I asked, while embracing my mother for the first time in a long while.

This was Alba's first visit to the United States of America. My mother would finally meet her other grandchildren Sofia and Gabriela.

John was very cordial toward my mother and welcomed her visit. My mother also seemed to move comfortably into the family routines. Her observations about her granddaughters started almost immediately.

"Pilar, I think Sofia is just like you, always getting into trouble," she laughed.

"Yeah, mom, I think you are right. She is a handful" I smiled.

I wanted my mother's visit to be a special one. Maybe I was moving too fast or too hard, but there was never any indication of stress between us on that visit. So, after settling in we decided to take Mama to Las Vegas. It was the first time she'd ever seen something so

PILAR

completely American. She was *all eyes,* as she absorbed the electric wonders of the Neon City.

It was fun watching her enjoy the experience, as she asked many questions and commenting on everything, like a little girl. "What's that? How did they do that? What's that made out of? Who owns this?" And, so on. I'm sure she had never seen anything like it and I had never really seen this side of her until now.

Growing up, my mother had never really given me much praise or encouragement. Now, it was like the floodgates of a mother's love had been released.

"Pilar I am so proud of all you have accomplished. You married a wonderful man. You have two beautiful daughters and live in this lovely house." I could hear the pride in her voice as she looked at me. It was the first time I heard any words come from my mother's mouth that were not angry, critical or admonishments.

Part of her blossoming was due to the fact that she really enjoyed being with her granddaughters. It felt good to spend some quality time with my mother and to let her see me in a new, mature light. I could feel her pride that I had not turned out too badly.

I particularly loved the family talks, when all of us, especially the girls, could get together and chat. Sometimes, though, the conversations would take turns that were unexpected. During one of these moments, my mom casually told us of the violence that was so common in Colombia and how hard it was to get a decent job. From what we read in the papers and saw on television, we agreed that it clearly was getting worse than even I remembered.

"Your aunt and cousins are struggling too. All of our lives are surrounded by so much drugs and crime."

It made it hard for us to visit such a dangerous place. I didn't want my daughters to be subjected to that violence and danger, but I longed to have family connections, and I think that it may have helped the girls appreciate their American life.

John and I discussed different ways we could change the situation, especially for my immediate family, but everything seemed so complicated and costly.

PILAR

Eventually, the visit ended and my mother returned to Colombia. We saw the short time we spent as only as a very pleasant visit. I know my mother had a really nice time and the subject was not brought up again, even as she was leaving to return home.

"Mom, give my love to the family and I will call you soon," I said to her as I was leaving the airport lobby.

Through my daily phone calls to my family in Colombia, I knew my sister, Carmen, was struggling with her addictions. She really wanted to get clean for herself and her children and provide a better life for them.

"I did it! I finally did it," she exclaimed during one of these calls. "I am clean, Pilar!" Her voice was so filled with hope and promise.

"I knew you could do it. I am so happy for you Carmen. This could be the beginning of a new life for you and the children."

"Yeah, I know, but I am so tired all the time. This job is so demanding. I feel so weak. Everything is such a struggle and David is such a handful," she explained.

"Carmen, go to the doctor, maybe he can give you something to help you." I advised.

Carmen was in sales for an insurance company. She would have to walk house-to-house, working long hours for very little pay. Eventually she took the time to see a doctor. He suggested she take a little time off, and that maybe a vacation would do her good.

All of a sudden, she made one of her most impetuous, yet sober decisions. "Pilar, the doctor said a vacation would do me good. I am taking three weeks off!"

Because I had noticed the change in her, I was not worried in the least and rejoiced, "Oh great! We should celebrate. Why don't you plan on coming out and visiting with us? You can meet your nieces, Sofia and Gabriela. They will be so excited to meet their tia."

I spoke with John about Carmen's visit and he was all for it.

"I love the idea," he said simply.

We started immediately planning for her visit. She told me in our next conversation that she had made arrangements to leave her children, Carolina and David with our mom. This would be a time for Carmen to be free of any obligations. She could really enjoy herself and relax in a way that she'd never done before and we'd be together like we hadn't had a chance to do since we were young children.

This visit to the U.S. would turn out to be the best three weeks of my sister's life.

The excitement started from the moment we spotted her at the airport. It was as if we were being given a gift of time that had been kept away from both our grasps for too long.

We took her to all the tourist spots including Disneyland. She was like a child in a candy store. I loved seeing her so happy.

On one short side trip, we went to San Diego.

On another, we took her to Las Vegas. We ate in fine restaurants and shopped till we dropped. The days we spent at home, we would go to Laguna Beach everyday, because I lived so close to the beach. I bonded with my sister for the first time in our lives.

She adored my girls and played with them often. Carmen was genuinely happy for my success. She hoped someday she would meet someone as caring as John and have a nice home. The sibling rivalries of our childhood were non-existent. There was no jealousy attached to her good wishes for our continued happiness and success. We had many chats on our trips to the beach. We discussed fashion, men, family etc., all the things that, an in the special way sisters long for. I felt so much closer to her during this time.

But never, ever did the situation with my father come up. Of course, at that time, that particular memory had not surfaced, it was still dormant. I realize it may have not revealed itself to my sister either. Anyway, the subject was never discussed and I am glad that it did not stain this wonderful memory.

The day before she left I took her shopping. I bought so many things for her and her family that I also had to buy an extra piece of luggage, just to pack everything for the return trip! There was this one particular dress she fell in love with. It had a handkerchief style hemline and Carmen just lit up when she tried it on. I was filled with joy seeing my sister so very happy. I knew we would miss her. We had such a grand time.

As I watched her take off I had an unsettling feeling. I guess I felt she was safe while with us. I knew, however that Colombia meant going back to a hard place to live and work.

PILAR

When Carmen arrived in Bogotá airport, she was waiting for another flight to Pereira. Amid the scrambling of people and general airport hustle, the television had breaking news. A woman had a bomb strapped to her neck and the bomb squad was on its way to disengage the bomb. At the same time I was getting the same news flash in the U.S.

We both watched in horror, from different countries, as the bomb exploded and killed not only the woman but also two of the members from the bomb squad. The difference was that in the United States this was an unthinkable crime. In Colombia it was all too easily accepted as an everyday part of life.

That's it, I thought. *I have got to get them out of Colombia. It's too dangerous.*

All day long I tried to get the picture of the woman with the bomb strapped to her neck, out of my head. I couldn't wait for John to get home. When he did arrive, I rushed to him at the door before he had a chance to close it.

"John, did you see the news flash from Bogotá?" I asked as the front door closed.

"Yeah, it's bad." He answered shaking his head.

As told to BARBARA RICH

"My family is in danger. We have to get them out of there somehow," I said, looking at him pleadingly. He looked down at me and you could see in his eyes that he sensed my concern.

"Let's think about it and see what we can do," he said thoughtfully.

We needed paperwork signed releasing full custody of David before we could have him leave the country.

John and I arranged the paperwork for Carlos to release legal custody of his son to Carmen. He did not leave the house, but gladly signed the document for which we paid him four hundred dollars. This document prohibited him from ever seeking any rights of parenthood, or decision making in the raising of David. The sum of four hundred dollars was Carlos's suggestion. There must have been an outstanding, unpaid bill in that amount. Carlos never seemed to think beyond the immediacy of his actions. It was worth every penny.

Eight months later my mother, Carmen, Carolina, David and Santiago were on a plane bound for Barcelona, Spain. The cost was monumental to cover moving, airline tickets

PILAR

and all the arrangements needed to complete this move from Colombia to Spain.

John and I had been sending about eight hundred to nine hundred dollars a month to cover expenses while my family was living in Colombia. Now we still had to support them when they arrived in Barcelona. It took about a year before my family could stand on their own. We had assumed the role of family caretakers, which would last for many years. This was made possible, thanks to John.

He never complained and we both seemed to accept the responsibility as a matter of course in our life together. I'm sure that there were hidden stresses, but we never spoke of them and life was peaceful for a while. I felt comfortable knowing my family was safe, but I did miss them. About two years later, things were going smoothly and John and I decided it was about time for us to spend Christmas with my family in Barcelona.

It would be the only Christmas we would all spend together, and what a Christmas it turned out to be. I remember the shopping and wrapping of all the gifts with such a childlike anticipation and joy, that was unlike any other that I'd ever had. The gathering of my family at the table as we ate and chatted of happy times, was food for the soul and I felt fed and blessed and satisfied like perhaps I'd never had before.

While the trip was spontaneous, it was not without planning, and after buying a big tree and placing in the corner of my mother's living room, I remember coming downstairs and seeing the smiling faces of my family light up, as the gifts were open. It is something that will live in my heart forever, and right at that moment I remember thinking that my heart was full. This wonderful holiday season spent together seemed to heal all the wounds of the past.

Two days before we left to return home, I took Carmen out to dinner. Understandably her son David was very angry and made a big fuss about her leaving him. As usual, his acting out seemed out of proportion to the situation, and maybe all of our patience had been worn thin for him. All I knew is that I just wanted to have a quiet dinner with my sister. We told David we wouldn't be long and to stay with Uncle John. Eventually we got out of the house and left.

PILAR

It was a beautiful night and we secured a nice table at the restaurant. We ordered some drinks and dinner, as if we had been doing this sort of thing all along. The atmosphere was such that we were able to open up with each other in a way that perhaps we never had before. "Ah, this is nice Pilar. This is just what I needed. I am so stressed out. I don't want to lose my job, but I keep taking time off because David is always getting into trouble and not paying attention. His grades are at such a low level. When he is at home he still takes so much out of me. I give in to him because I just get tired of fighting with him. Sometimes I think it would be best to just give him to the state," she confessed.

"Carmen, you don't mean that. Right now you are really stressed and everything seems so much worse. It will get better," I said trying to console her.

"I know you must think I'm a terrible mother, Pilar, but I just can't take it anymore."

I really didn't know what to say to her. "Carmen, we are here now having a nice dinner. Just try to enjoy this time together." We changed the subject and talked about a number of other things.

As told to BARBARA RICH

When we got back home, John complained about David's behavior.

"David went crazy when you left," John said, somewhat shocked. "He started kicking me and screaming that you took his mother away from him. He was out of control, so I put him in his room for time out."

I don't know what made me do it. Maybe it was a feeling of support and appreciation for John that was beyond any of my new joy I was experiencing with my sister, but I turned to my sister and said, "Gee, Carmen can't you control your own child? You are the adult. He's the child. You can't give in to him all the time."

Perhaps I left her no room for any other reaction, but she got very defensive and offended by my remark, which was probably insensitive especially after her confession during dinner, the content of which was now completely forgotten. We also both conveniently forgot that the probable cause of David's strange behavior was the fact that Carmen had used drugs all during her pregnancy.

"He's my son, I can handle him. Just leave him alone!"

PILAR

"Look Carmen, You just can't give him everything he wants," I raised my voice and sounded like I knew what I was talking about.

"He is my son, Pilar. I will handle it!"
The truth of the matter was, Carmen was so stressed and exhausted she simply surrendered to his demands rather than try to discipline him.

"O.K. fine Carmen. He is your son," I said calmly.

Carmen remained cordial but very quiet for the rest of our visit. The underlying hurt was still stinging from my remarks about David. We managed to get through the next couple of days before our departure without incident, but it was obvious that something had changed. The abandoned joy was gone and a nagging tension was beginning to creep back into our relationship.

Finally we said our goodbyes and boarded our flight back to the states. I looked at my sister before I left, trying to clear my heart of any tensions, but something would not let me relax. I was disturbed. I wished I could take back what I had said because I knew that I would never want to hurt her. It is very hard for me to write about it even now. My heart was no longer full, and the emptiness was probably of my own doing. I'll never get over the fact that this would be the only Christmas we would all be together.

When we got back I wasn't comfortable with the way things were left unsaid between my sister and I, so I called Carmen. We had a long conversation and I told her how much I loved her. She was very receptive.

"Carmen, you are my only sister," I said. "I want us to stay close and always be able to talk to one another."

"I love you too, Pilar and don't worry I am not angry or hurt. I know you were only trying to help me. It is just that I am so exhausted all the time," she said.

I felt better after hearing her voice. All was forgiven and things were good again between us. I continued to keep in touch with my family in Barcelona as usual. Around March when I called, it seemed I never got to speak with my sister.

"Hola mama, donde esta Carmen?" I asked.

"Oh Carmen, she is taking a nap. She is very tired," she replied.

The next time I called it would be something else.

PILAR

"Mama, let me speak to Carmen."

"She is not here now. She had to go to the store." My mother would always respond with some excuse why Carmen could not come to the phone. She became less and less available to talk to me. *Was it because of my insensitive remarks?* I wondered.

It was already April and I wanted to know what was going on. I had also stayed in communication with my brother and I decided to call Pedro and ask him if there was any sign that what I'd said had affected my relationship with Carmen.

"Hola Pedro, que paso con Carmen?" I asked

"Pilar, Carmen is not doing well, she is always tired and very weak. I feel so sorry for her," was his answer.

"Well has she been to a doctor? Something must be wrong. She needs to find out why she is always so tired," I added, concerned.

"I know, but she won't go. She is afraid to take off any more work and then David is putting such a strain on her. She can't afford to lose her job."

"Well I just have to talk to her and tell her she must see a doctor. This has been going on for too long."

"O.K. Pilar. Try to get a hold of her and talk to her. Maybe she will listen to you."

I hung up the phone and tried again to call Carmen. Finally, she answered the phone.

"Hola, Carmen. How are you feeling? I haven't spoken to you in such a long time. Are you alright?" I asked, glad to hear her voice.

"Hola Pilar. I'm sorry. It's just that I am under so much stress. I am always tired and sometimes when I wake up there is blood in my throat and when I brush my teeth my gums bleed."

This was completely unexpected. My heart went out to her. I wished I could be there to comfort her. She needed professional help and I was so far away.

"Carmen, listen to me. You must see a doctor. You can't go on like this. I love you and I want you to get better. Please, make an appointment and just do it. Why go on suffering?"

"Alright Pilar; I will try. I promise."

PILAR

After that conversation, I was in daily contact with my family, always checking to see how Carmen was progressing.

"Carmen what did the doctor say?" That was how most of the conversations began.

"Oh, they took blood tests, so we will see what they find. I just feel so weak all the time," she usually answered.

"Well at least now we can find out what's going on. I am anxious to see what the tests show. I will call you tomorrow. Try and rest."

"O.K. I will try," She responded, noticeably weaker, even over the telephone.

This went on from the end of April, through May. On May 25th Carmen got a call from the doctor telling her to get to the hospital immediately because he wanted to run more critical tests. He told her the initial results were disturbing and her condition needed attention as soon as possible.

She had just gotten the word from the doctor when I had made my nightly call. She told me exactly what the doctor had said and she sounded very slightly frightened and extremely overwhelmed. "Carmen, you get to the hospital the first thing tomorrow. We need

As told to BARBARA RICH

to find out exactly what is the problem. Please make sure you get there right away." I was both forcibly telling and gently begging her. My heart was pounding with the urgency the doctor expressed.

"Pilar, first I have to go to a meeting at the school for David. Carolina will come with me. After that I will go to the hospital and undergo further tests."

I was restless the whole day. My mind was taking me places I didn't want to go.

It was a good thing my life was busy with my girls. It temporarily took my mind away from the worries about Carmen, but not for long. After they were in bed, I prayed and prayed for a reasonable solution to whatever it was that was stealing the strength from my sister.

The next day, May 26th Carmen was diagnosed with stage five leukemia. This time I didn't have to call. My brother called me. I was stunned. I didn't want to believe it, but I knew in my heart it was going to be very serious.

From that moment onward, I would call her at the hospital everyday and try and lift her spirits. Her breathing became more and more labored and she sounded very weak.

PILAR

"Carmen, I am making arrangements to come to see you and take care of you when you get home. I will be there in July," I told her.

"Oh Pilar, I am so happy to hear that. I look forward to having you here with me. You know they shaved my head. I am bald!" she said with the most energy she could muster.

"Well, finally I can be the prettiest sister,' I teased. "When I come out there I will shop and get you a beautiful wig."

"Pilar, I want to see *mi Papa*. I want to at least talk to him. Can you see if you can find out where he is?" She asked.

I'm sure she wanted to tell our father that she was very ill and wanted to see him. I had not recalled any of the hidden abuse at that time.

"I will check into it Carmen and let him know. You just rest now. I will be there soon," I encouraged. I hung up the phone and made a few calls in an attempt to locate my absentee father, but no luck locating him in Spain or Colombia.

After that, my focus was mainly on getting prepared for my trip. I planned on staying with her for about three weeks. I basically would be her caretaker when she got home.

Carmen was getting very aggressive treatment because of the stage five cancer. She also was getting a very advanced treatment from the United States. As is often the case with this kind of therapies, it was as if the cure was worse than the disease. These treatments took so much out of her. She was so weak when I called, that she could hardly talk. My heart ached for her.

The phone calls now were mostly the sound of her crying on one end and me trying to stifle my sobs at the other, with very few words being spoken. Through all the treatment though, she never mentioned anything about dying. She would just say the treatment made her so sick, but she never seemed to give up hope.

Finally after what seemed like forever, I had made all my arrangements and purchased my tickets to Barcelona for a trip in July. It was only June now but I felt a little better knowing that I would be there soon.

On June 22nd, Pedro called. "Pilar, You must come quickly. Carmen has been placed in

PILAR

I.C.U. Her condition has worsened. She is very, very ill."

"Oh my God," I thought. *"What can I do? I already have reservations."*

"Pedro, fax me a note from the doctor stating Carmen's condition and the urgency to change my reservations for tomorrow. Please do it right away!"

"I'll do it right away. Hopefully we will see you tomorrow," He said and hung up the phone so quickly that I could feel his urgency in the sudden silence.

It took twenty-four hours to complete the transfer of my tickets. The whole time my head was spinning. I also had to make arrangements for my girls and get ready quickly. I didn't even check any luggage. I just brought a carry-on. Anxiety kept me going despite my total exhaustion. To make matters worse, I had to take a *red-eye* flight.

My flight landed at about midnight and Pedro was eagerly waiting like a drowning man looks to the lifeguard to rescue him. *If only I could change the impending condition of my sister,* I thought when I saw him. We embraced and took a taxi to the house.

As told to BARBARA RICH

Mama, Carolina, David and Santiago (Carolina's son) were there to welcome me. We talked until three o'clock in the morning. None of us could sleep. Finally we realized we had to get some rest if we were going to the hospital first thing in the morning. We made an attempt to try and get some sleep. David and I shared my sister's room. There were two twin beds in her room, so David, now eleven, slept in the bed next to me. I was dozing off, and then I opened my eyes about 4 o'clock. I couldn't say what woke me up, but David also woke up and said he couldn't sleep, either. We got up and one by one everybody was gathered again in one room. It was clear we were just not going to get any sleep.

About six o'clock the hospital called informing us to come as quickly as possible. Carmen's condition was worse than before and was being called, "Very grave."

We all scurried about making arrangements for David and Santiago to stay with a neighbor. The hospital did not allow children in the Intensive Care Unit.

"David and Santiago, you can't come to the hospital. You will have to stay with the next store neighbor till we return. We will give a hug and kiss to your mama and grandma for you," I said, trying to comfort them. Luckily, the extreme seriousness of the situation caused them both to accept my authority and they agreed to behave.

We arrived at St. Paulo Hospital, one of the best in the area about seven-thirty a.m. Pedro led the way into the I.C.U. The doctor was just leaving Carmen's room when he recognized Pedro from when he saw him on previous visits.

"I'm sorry, Carmen just passed away," The doctor simply stated, as if he was reporting the weather.

We all heard what he said and were stunned. The moment is frozen in my mind, like a scene through an open window. I could not do, think or feel anything. I could not even cry. I was beyond numb. With great effort I turned slightly and saw Mama and Carolina crying. There was another brief moment of disassociation and I saw Pedro and I suddenly trying to comfort them. Mama started to pull away.

"Mama," Pedro pleaded. "Please don't go in her room! Remember her the way she was when she was well."

As told to BARBARA RICH

I wondered to myself why, in her brief life, Carmen had so few well and happy times. It seemed she went from drugs to pregnancy to illness. She was always struggling.

"Pedro, I will go in with Carolina," I said, still numb. "You stay with Mama."

Carolina and I entered her room like phantom shells, almost zombie like. Entering the death room of a loved one is indescribable. All emotion, thoughts and memories have boiled to the point that they almost eliminate sound. Sorrow of this magnitude is like a black hole. Nothing escapes, not even sound.

The moment is captured, therefore in my soul like the tragic painting of a master artist. We approached Carmen's bed slowly, as if gliding along the floor. We stood side-by-side holding hands then Carolina reached out, and let her hand hover just above her mother's arm for a fragment of time. Imperceptibly her hand sank down and silently touched her mother's cold body. She began to cry.

When I saw Carmen she was hardly recognizable. I could see the pain chiseled into her stone-cold face from all the suffering she had been through. Her whole body was swollen and there were tubes in her nose. Blood was on her face. It was one of the most horrific sights I'd ever witnessed. Strangely, still I could not cry.

When we left her room the doctor and a social services person expressed their condolences and asked the family if we would be having an autopsy. We all agreed to have an autopsy done to know exactly what happened. It was like watching from afar during these conversations at the hospital. I was still in shock. As I watched them transport my sister's body in a zipped body bag to the morgue for an autopsy, it still didn't seem real to me.

When we finally left the hospital, we all went to a nearby cafeteria to grab a cup of coffee and discuss what we needed to do and how to break the news to Carmen's son, David. There were so many, many phone calls to make. We also need to call David's school psychologist and ask her the best way to handle David. There were many details that needed to be considered, and David was just one of the more pressing.

Everyone was stunned to hear of Carmen's death. They all expressed that they thought she had more time. We had all been taking our cues from Carmen and I guess even she thought she could hang on longer. She was so confident in fact, that she had never expressed her wishes for her funeral arrangements, or what kind of service there should be. We really had no way of knowing what she wanted and perhaps we had all fallen into the many traps of denial.

No one was taking the lead and I just couldn't deal with any funeral arrangements. It just seemed like a confirmation of her death, and I was not ready for that. Finally, Pedro took on that responsibility and made all the funeral arrangements. Carmen did not have life insurance, but she had taken out a policy for funeral expenses about six months previously.

When we returned home our heads were spinning with all that needed to be done and what was the best way to get them done.

"Donde esta la Mama?' asked David, his eyes searching for an answer.

"Your Mama is in Heaven, David. She won't be sick anymore," I told him, while I embraced him.

"Como esta Tita?' cried Santiago. Tita was the name he called his grandma. Santiago was very sad.

PILAR

In between phone calls and decisions we had to make for David, we did little else but cry and sleep. This went on for several days. John called and asked me if I would be returning sooner since the death of my sister was so sudden. I had originally planned to stay three weeks.

"No, John, I am going to stay the full time. There is so much that needs to be done and I want to be here to help. Are the girls alright?" I asked.

"Sofia and Gabriela are fine." He answered calmly. "Stay, and take care of whatever you need to do. I'm so sorry Pilar. I know this didn't turn out the way you expected."

I knew he was disappointed, but he said that he understood.

David's behavior was more strange than usual. He always needed attention, but now it seemed worse. It was exhausting.

The day of the funeral was a little shocking. When they took the family in the room to see Carmen, she was laid out in a nun's habit. This was customary at a Catholic funeral, if no other requests were made, and since

Carmen could not express her wishes, she was laid out dressed as a nun.

David kept going over to the casket and lifting the viewing lid while hugging his mother. It almost seemed to me that he wanted people to notice him. We found out later that while Carmen was hospitalized, David had a conversation with her. David had made some request that his mother couldn't give him.

The last words David said to his mother were, "I hope you die!" It turned out that these were words he can never take back. To this day it still haunts him.

When we arrived at the church it seemed I was just placing one foot in front of the other as we entered through the doors. I was barely aware of the scent of the flowers or the burning candles that permeated the chapel. My eyes lifted as I slowly noticed the pews were filled with so many people. There were about one hundred people. I wondered, *"Who are all these people?"*

At the church service the casket was closed, due to the manner in which Carmen had passed away. We wanted Carmen to be remembered as the beautiful woman she was before this horrid disease stole her essence.

PILAR

Carmen's co-workers made up the bulk of the congregation. They had checked in with us during her illness to ask how she was doing. Some of them had even given blood. "Blood," I thought. While the blood was flowing through my veins I couldn't help but think of the poisonous venom that had been pumped in the veins of my sister that eventually stole her life.

As I became more and more aware of my surroundings, I finally came to grips with the fact that my sister was gone. My grief was still raw because it was painfully clear that I would never have the opportunity to embrace her again. I can picture her face and the times we shared together. I know I will visit those memories often. The sorrow would grow distant in time, but the love I felt would remain forever vivid in my heart.

One of the many decisions that had to be made was to have my sister cremated, how it was going to happen and who would be witness. Only two people were to be admitted to the cremation. It was decided that Pedro and Carolina were the two who would stay during the process. As I watched Pedro and Carolina walk toward the cremation room, something stirred in me, and when they closed the door it was like the sound of an ancient tomb separating us for all eternity. I stood there with my mother and just like a dam of collected sorrows bursting after so much pressure, my tears came and I finally cried. I had tried to be the strong one for everyone. I had always taken care of my family and tried to protect them. Now, there was nothing I could do.

I felt that David and Carolina should make the decision of what to do with the ashes. What they decided was fitting I felt. After I left Spain, they took the ashes to the ocean near where we had grown up. My mother, Pedro, and the two children were there. My brother, I was told, opened the urn and threw them toward the water, but the wind shifted, leaving him with a mouthful of my sister's remains.

After the funeral, we returned home and the grieving continued as we tried to make decisions that would be best for everyone, especially David. Pedro decided to give up his apartment and move back in with our mom and raise David. After all, David was not only the son of his sister, but also the son of his lover.

How ironic, I thought, that Pedro would ultimately raise David. Carmen would have been very upset. David was the last person she would have wanted to be in Pedro's care. To this day I have never mentioned to Pedro how Carmen still resented him for arguments in the past. Pedro was the last person to see her alive. He visited her daily and still it was Carmen who held on to their past.

Pedro on the other hand raised David as he would his own son and is still a great part of his life.

I'd like to believe and I do, that deep down Carmen loved Pedro with all her heart and she just had a hard time letting go of memories in her head. It turned out Pedro was the best choice and I know she wanted the best for David.

Tons of paperwork (again the paperwork!) was necessary to complete and finalize these arrangements. So now, Pedro would be living with David, Santiago, Carolina and our mother. There was so much going on that the three weeks that I'd originally scheduled for my trip, just flew by.

Oddly, it never occurred to me that my father was still missing. He had not attended the funeral, just as he had been absent when Carmen passed, even though she had asked about him. His absence should have been obvious and probably draw some attention, but no one mentioned it or seemed to care.

Leaving my family in Barcelona was difficult, but I missed my daughters and my husband and wanted to get back to them and the other obligations I left behind. I have learned that no matter how horribly your heart is breaking, the world does not stop for your grief.

The trip home would be a long one. I had two connecting flights. As I boarded my second flight from London to New York, I became restless and nervous as I made my way through the plane searching for my seat. I could feel my heart pounding. When we took off, I tried to calm myself, but events of the last three weeks came flooding to my mind.

"If only I had gone straight to the hospital, maybe Carmen would have seen me and...." I trailed off in my thoughts. *"Oh what does it matter now? Carmen is dead."*

I could feel my pulse racing. I couldn't breath. Finally I got up and walked to the flight attendant.

"I can't breath and my heart is pounding," I managed to say. She immediately got me some oxygen and placed me in first-class. It calmed me down a little bit but thoughts came in and out as I recalled the last three weeks. I remained with the oxygen for the remainder of the flight, which was four hours. I must commend the staff on British Airways for their immediate and perceptive response and concern to make me comfortable.

John met me at the airport and we held each other. "How did it go? He asked.

"Oh John it was horrible, just so sad," I answered still clinging to him.

"The girls are anxious to see you. I know you will feel better after you see them. They have really missed you." He said, as we headed toward the car.

The drive from the airport was somber and uneventful. As I entered the house, I realized how much I missed being home. The girls came running to me, their arms opened. Their hugs and kisses were like drugs to an addict. They asked about their aunt Carmen and Carolina. I tried to tell them how sad I was, without scaring them. I wanted them to remember their aunt with loving thoughts. To their credits they handled the sad news with grace and poise.

Days went by as I tried to get back to my usual routine, but it was very hard. In my moments alone I would cry. Finally, I decided to see a therapist. She helped me get through the first couple of weeks. John knew I was still very sad and he didn't understand why I was still so sad.

"Honey, I thought you would be doing better after three weeks," he said.

"Oh John you have never lost anyone. You have no idea how traumatic this was for me," I said, trying to explain my sorrow that I even I did not understand fully.

"I'm sorry, Pilar. I just want you to feel better," he added, trying to comfort me.

"I'm not ready John. It takes time. I don't know what to tell you. I'm trying to move on the best I can."

I was still incredibly sensitive in my grief. It was like a wound that all things, even medicines, seem to irritate. In time, I would learn to cope and prioritize my family's happiness over the sorrow.

PILAR

As told to BARBARA RICH

Chapter eight
Pedro as Caretaker

I called often to see how Pedro was doing with David. I knew David would be tough to control. After all, he was a product of parents who used drugs and alcohol and were not, perhaps given the best skills of child rearing by their own parents. It's one of those vicious cycles we hear so much about.

"Pilar, David is making me crazy. He is so hard to handle. I need a break," Pedro pleaded. It was approaching the first anniversary of Carmen's passing.

"Pedro maybe we can arrange for David to spend the summer here with us," I offered.

"Oh Pilar, that would be great." He sighed heavily at the thought of a possibility of relief. "You have no idea how much this would mean to me!"

As usual John and I footed the bill and made arrangements for David to come stay with us the entire summer. Pedro was more objective about Carmen's death. He never had that bond that I had with my sister. For the most part he resented her betrayal with his lover and their having a child together. In addition to David being a constant reminder of that betrayal, I'm sure handling David didn't give him much time for anything else.

David's stay with us was hectic. I now had a better understanding of what both Carmen and Pedro were dealing with. Sofia and Gabriela made a fuss over David. We took him to all the fun places and bought him tons of clothes. He was treated very well.

One night I placed a picture of his mother on the night table next to his bed.

"David, I know you miss your mother and she loved you so much. I thought you would like this picture of her. She was so beautiful," I said, trying to see if I could get a response from him. He said nothing. The next day he had removed the picture of his mother and replaced it with the fish from the movie "Finding Nemo." This is a story about a fish searching for its mother. I thought that was odd, at the time but I realize now the significance. David, indeed, was quite a challenge and none of us were really qualified to understand him.

As told to BARBARA RICH

The visit ended without any problems, per se but the constant stress of knowing that a blow-up at any moment was possible, made John and I tense and uncomfortable. With mixed feelings we set out to the airport for David's departure. I was relieved to be rid of the burden of having David stay with us, but also had concerns for his mental and emotional stability. It was a grim reminder of the stress that was put upon my sister. I ached for both of them. I also knew that Pedro would have a rough road ahead caring for David.

"Thanks again, Pilar for taking such good care of David. I'm sure this is a trip he will always remember," he said, as he looked at the suitcase full of clothes and gifts for everyone.

I chatted awhile with Pedro and told him of the incident with the picture of Carmen and how David replaced it with the fish from Finding Nemo. Pedro knew there were problems ahead and was willing to try and make things better.

"Oh, by the way, before I forget, guess who called?" he questioned. He answered quickly, indicating that he did not really want a response. "Papa. That's right, he called from prison in Colombia. He said he knew about Carmen when she was sick, but couldn't get away. More drug trafficking. Can you believe it?"

My heart just sank. Until that moment I had totally forgotten about my father.

"Nothing surprises me about Papa!" I spat out the words because the thought of him was distasteful to me. "I feel bad for Carmen though, because she wanted to see him or at least talk with him. For me, the less I see or hear from him the better."

Now that David was back in Spain with Pedro, my life began to fall back into a comfortable, normal routine. I felt bad for David. Given the cards he was dealt, I did not see a bright future ahead of him. However, I suppressed the nagging guilt and immersed myself into life with my immediate family.

John's business was flourishing, which afforded us a chance to live well. We did a lot of traveling with our girls, Sofia and Gabriela. We went camping and hosted many barbecues. Sofia and Gabriela were involved in so many sports and also took piano lessons and bi-lingual classes. I was helping John with his business when I wasn't taking the girls from one event to another. Life was good. I felt I was living the American Dream. I found great comfort knowing we were giving our children a stable childhood. I wanted them to have everything I missed growing up.

Every so often ugly memories of Colombia and my cousin raping me would surface. I would go to therapy and talk about it. It haunted me like a heavy shadow hanging on my shoulders. I wondered when I would get over it.

The years passed with no major crisis and our life was typical of most families. We had our ups and downs, but for the most part, it was a full and happy life. After about sixteen years of marriage, I sensed a bit of a distance growing between John and me. It was nothing drastic. John was gone a great deal of the time on business and I had so much in my life, it almost played as a distraction when he was around, so that I didn't think much of our slowly drifting away from each other.

We had kept a practice of a date night once a week, when we would go to a nice restaurant and discuss Sofia and Gabriela or remodeling the house. I felt like we were becoming really good friends. Even though we were good friends who loved one another, John (like most married men I believed) wanted more intimacy and more attention, but my focus was mainly on my girls. I eventually went back to my therapist and told her I was depressed and quite often losing my temper. I didn't understand. I had everything I had hoped for: a good husband, two beautiful children, a beautiful home and we were all healthy.

The therapist suggested it was because of my childhood. At this time in my life, I had no revelation of the incest between my father and my sister. It was still buried very deep, below the surface, at the core of my being.

A very slow, downward regression was happening in my marriage--like that black hole drawing in the light--that would later explode with John's infidelity.

Every time I talked to Pedro, there were always problems. I tried to co-parent with him on David's behalf. I had two children of my own and I felt I could help, but David's needs were beyond my abilities. He needed a miracle, but I felt like I was all out of them. It seemed he was beyond human help.

Sadly, in a tangled web that I thought was unique and common to my life, my brother

As told to BARBARA RICH

Pedro had become the parent of his ex-lover's son armed only with the parenting skills he'd learned from his father. It was similar to being completely unarmed, thrust into a fight for your life and desperately trying to protect yourself, without any real weapons or ammunition.

However, I was so involved in the surface details of my own life (probably as a defense against actually dealing with deep seated wounds that were still festering) that I didn't pay much attention to Pedro's problems or other danger signs in my relationship with John.

PILAR

As told to BARBARA RICH

Chapter nine
My In-laws

A very domineering mother raised my husband. She was also not one to show affection to her children. John's mother had another son from a previous marriage, but John's half-brother was not raised in the same household.

Her son from her first marriage remained with his father after the divorce and consequently remained distant from John. John also had a younger brother, but they were not close either. When it came to his family history it was like John was a secret agent, or possibly in the witness protection program. He never talked much about it.

The story that I was able to piece together begins with the fact that at age eighteen he left for college and did very well. This was not unusual, as many young people leave the nest at this time and seek their own identity.

John is a very intelligent man. After college he took a special course abroad at the

PILAR

University of Madrid, Spain. He picked up the language quickly and by the second year he was teaching English while in Spain. It afforded him the luxury of seeing Europe. He traveled extensively and enjoyed his stay abroad. When he returned to New York he started teaching there and of course, that is when we met and were later married.

After we wed we came to California for a few days and I met John's parents. From day one we had problems. I found my new mother-in-law to be self-centered and very arrogant. She resented me from the start. Nothing I could do would please her and she didn't seem that thrilled with her son's decisions either. She found fault with everything John and I did. She even implied that we "made a mistake" having two daughters. She thought we should have had sons like her instead of our two girls.

I'm not sure how she treated John before I came into the picture, but I had a sneaking suspicion that her tact and subtlety was abandoned at the very moment when I walked through the door. John appeared shocked at some of the things she said to him, and to me and I believe he was embarrassed by her behavior, but unable to really act against his mother's wishes.

It was as if she wanted to punish John for marrying me. She did not like the fact that John had married any woman without her approval, but I served up several delicate problems for her. She was not happy that I was Spanish and did not speak refined English. She had mentioned that most college boys married their college sweethearts and usually looked for a woman who was "like their mother."

Kitty, John's mom, was petite and very conscience of her appearance. She always dressed very well. I got the feeling she thought she was above everyone else. She was always mistreating me and her verbal abuse stung at the core. I didn't know where she thought John would find such a woman. It never occurred to me that I was somehow fulfilling a need in my husband that was not being met when he left home.

"Your mother is crazy, John," I told him, full of anger and contempt. "Can't you defend us?"

"You're right, Pilar. I can hardly stand to be with her myself," he answered looking defeated. "But, she's my mother. I don't know what else to do except limit our time with her. The less time spend with her the better." John wanted to avoid confrontation, so he preferred to just to stay away.

John's dad on the other hand was very pleasant toward me and always tried to make me feel welcome. He never said much. I thought, *"How could he stand to be with Kitty who was always, not only totally dominating the conversations but seemed to demand that the very life energy of the room be directed toward her?"* I'm sure, as with John the dad wanted to avoid confrontation.

Kitty was not your typical grandmother, either. She might have been with her grandchildren ten times in fourteen years. When she was with them she was more partial to one than the other and made it obvious. There was no real reason for this favoritism that I could see, since the girls both treated their paternal grandmother with love and kindness.

Her behavior really upset me. At one point, during one of her strained visits I finally got up the nerve to tell her to leave.

"I don't know why you are treating my daughters so differently or why you seem to hate me, but I've had enough. You have to go."

As told to BARBARA RICH

She did not argue the point or try to defend herself. Perhaps she knew that my assessment of her behavior was accurate and she had no intention of changing. We did not speak for ten years. It was a great relief for me. Years passed and Kitty called John to tell him that his father had passed away. About that time she made a meager attempt to make amends for her behavior in the past. She wanted to let us know she was proud of what we had accomplished through the years and was more accepting of me. I still didn't feel it was a genuine apology. I suspected she had some kind of a personality disorder, but like most patients and people who have their own emotional problems I've started to think I know as much about mental illness as the experts. I see this happen a lot with alcoholics and addicts who are becoming sober. I guess it's easier to see the failings of others than to admit our own.

PILAR

As told to BARBARA RICH

Chapter ten
My Parents

What I dreaded most was to have a relationship like my mother and father had. My father put my mother through a living hell. I wanted no part of it. I wanted my daughters to have everything I had missed in my childhood and more. The more I faced the horrors of my past, the more I had to accept that I was, like John, a product of my parents. To heal myself completely, I needed to face the sickness of my parent's relationship with one another.

First I needed to make peace with the past. I had to deal with the issues that were buried for so long. Becoming a mother made it easier to have compassion for my own mother. Raising children is a full time job and we do the best with what we know and have. I realize now, my mother's trauma in her life was at a different time and in a different country. She did the best she could do, given the circumstances. My father was her life. She never got over him, no matter how he treated her or her children. She struggled after he

PILAR

deserted us, trying to take care of us. She had some training while working in a salon earlier in her life. Finally, after a long struggle, she was able to use our living room as a salon to do hair. We weren't rich but we were doing all right. Her situation was overwhelming for that time. Coming to terms with a gay son, which was not accepted in those days, and a daughter that was into drugs were monumental issues to overcome, not to mention all the rest of it.

I can't imagine the pressure she had to endure while trying to make a modest living. My mother, now in her eighties, was in the early stages of Alzheimer's and my heart ached for her and the life she should and could have had if only she would have let go of what bound her to my father. She never stopped talking about him. The memories of the pain and embarrassment my mother suffered is forever etched in my mind. This is why I never want to live that kind of life. I felt closer to my mother as time went on, and hoped to visit her in Spain sometime soon.

My father, now that is another story. I *want* to forget all the horrible things he has done, but I know I never will. In fact, remembering those horrible things, took me on this journey in the first place. It caused me to face and deal with those buried issues. Through my pain, I know I have grown and developed an awareness and broader sense of understanding and sensibility. I have forgiven my father because I had to, for myself, more than for him. His behavior was deplorable and caused so much pain to so many people. My father, like my mother is also in his eighties and living in Spain. But as far as I am concerned has been dead to me for a long time. I didn't care if I ever saw or heard from him again.

    I had to go through stages of loss and grieving for the end of my marriage to John. At first, I felt vengeance had been served and I was free to do whatever I wanted. My girls always remained my first priority, but when I had my time, I spent it partying and gallivanting. I tried to put all the lost years of freedom from fun and capsulate it in a short time. Well, that was short lived. Eventually I became very, very depressed. I didn't know at the time that I was mourning a family unit that was now broken and separated.

    John and I were civil to one another for the sake of the children. I feel no animosity toward him.

PILAR

Money was an issue and my teenaged daughters needed my attention. They were also going through the usual painful transitions. I spent so much time crying. I was drowning myself in self-pity. Nothing could motivate me, but I had to move on. I knew it. Somehow I had to find the strength to pull myself together and find a job, get out of the house, meet people, start living again. I became more and more desperate because money matters were becoming monumental. I'd dig a ditch if I had to. Deep down inside, I knew I was strong. I had faced challenges far worse. I could do this. I had to.

Finally, I did get a job in a high-end resort hotel and I love it. Just being in the beautiful surroundings near the ocean was peace for my soul. Even as a child I always gravitated to the sea. I felt there *was* a light at the end of the tunnel. This would be the beginning of a new and happier period.

I look ahead to all the new challenges that are in store for me. I've met a wonderful man, who treats me well and gives me some stability. Everyone seems to like him, even John, my ex, approves and really likes him.

As told to BARBARA RICH

My daughters are still processing the divorce, but doing better. They are teenagers with normal teenage issues, which can be challenging at times, but we are making it through.

I continue on the path of recovery. This experience has brought me a new freedom. I know who I am. I feel I can handle anything that life may throw my way. It hasn't been easy. It's a long process healing not only my current divorce, but the buried past I have uncovered. I am proud of myself, as I become an example to my children of how I have handled life's struggles.

Life has not been easy for my brother Pedro either. Spain is going through an economic crisis. My native country has been hit hard. It has been very difficult trying to keep his small business of dry-cleaning afloat. He also cares for our mother, which is no small task. He cooks and prepares her meals and cleans up after her, making sure she is comfortable. David is now nineteen and living with his girlfriend in Barcelona. He visits Pedro and his grandma a few times a month. David is no longer the burden he had been while living with his uncle. Pedro tells me, when we talk on

PILAR

the phone, that David seems to be clean right now. Carolina, my sister's daughter is living in Canada with her son Santiago, who would be Carmen's grandson. They are trying to make a living there. It seems my brother has always been the caretaker. For ten years he raised my sister's children and grandchild. Now, at fifty-five he has no time for a personal life. He is in no committed relationship. There is no time. His main focus is caring for our mother and running his small business. He does have many friends he sees now and again. Through all this, he never complains to me about his life. He always has a positive outlook.

    Nine years have passed since the death of my sister, Carmen. I have so many family and friends from Barcelona, Colombia and here in the United States that have comforted me and been there during these trying times. They all mean so much to me. My journey through these times would have been beyond what I could handle without their love and support. Even though oceans separated us, they were only a phone call away. It made me feel like they were right here with me, during these trials in my life, like shelter in a storm.

As told to BARBARA RICH

As I turn the page on the next chapter of my life, I am filled with hope and freedom. I am willing to work hard to achieve a positive and productive lifestyle for my children and myself. Even though I have less material things, I am free from anxiety and filled with peace. I am grateful to have overcome the struggles and trials of my life until now. It has prepared me to accept and deal with any trials that may be in the future. I have a clear focus of what is important in my life and will strive toward its fruition.

PILAR

As told to BARBARA RICH

Chapter eleven
Healing

I can feel the weight of the past, like a huge boulder, lifting from me as I embark on the future. I am willing to work hard to achieve a positive and productive lifestyle for my children and myself. The previous struggles and hardships have well prepared me for any trials that might lie ahead. If I might borrow a phrase from the song, "what doesn't kill you, makes you stronger."

My shoes are well worn from pounding the pavement while looking for work. I was out of the workforce for several years and as a single mom, it was hard to get back into the rhythm. The many interviews seemed endless, but finally I was able to secure a job. Thankful once again that I am bi-lingual, I am sure that was an integral part in finding a position fairly easily.

At one point I had to take two jobs to make ends meet. As difficult as that was, the freedom and peace within me made it tolerable.

PILAR

One night, while out with a girlfriend grabbing a bit to eat, a pleasant looking gentlemen approached our table and made conversation. His name was Dennis and after awhile we exchanged phone numbers. I do believe it was divine intervention, because I was definitely not on the hunt for a man in my life. I was rapt in caring for my girls and trying to keep my head above water. A man in my life was on a back burner waiting to be lit sometime in the future. I felt as if I had finally gained a firm foothold on what once was a sheer cliff and I was beginning to find that stable plateau. But, life surprises you when you least expect it.

Dennis did call and we dated a few times. Our relationship had all the initial elements, attraction, sex etc. I was reluctant to be exclusive and our relationship was open and honest.

Before we had committed to each other seriously I gave Dennis a copy of the manuscript that you are reading. He read it in private and when he came back he said, "I am very sorry you've gone through so much in your life, Pilar." Tears were just behind his eyes. "I am willing to continue seeing you, on a more exclusive basis...if you want to...with one condition." I took a deep breath, not knowing what was coming next. "Never make me a salad, please." This is still the source of humor in our ongoing relationship.

When I embarked on the road to recovery from my haunted past, I found myself in another struggle: because of my eagerness to be independent and find work to provide and sustain a life for me and my daughters, I made the mistake of drinking heavily at the end of every day.

I soon became a slave to my alcohol. Obviously, I had fallen into the trap of believing you can substitute one addiction for another and if you do you're not really addicted.

In a short time, it became a major focus of my daily existence. Obviously I had the genetic disposition for abuse in my DNA. My father was an alcoholic and both my siblings had issues with alcohol and drugs. I had abused alcohol in the past...pretending that I had a good excuse. My health deteriorated and became worse with time. I called in sick many times on the job, often because I was really sick. My immune system was shot, and the

PILAR

alcohol didn't help. Eventually, I went to the doctor to see what could be done.

"Pilar you need to detox." Dr. Hogan said calmly, but with real concern.

I knew he was right, but I hated the thought of going through the pain of withdrawal. So, I faced another hurdle in my life.

I tried A.A. for a while. I just couldn't do it by myself, and the support that I had from my loved ones was not enough.

I know what I have been through and I know I can overcome this next hurdle. I looked at the doctor with hope rather than despair and said. "I can do this. Whatever it takes I will do."

I did not know how hard it would be to keep to this promise. Things have gone from bad to worse with John. One recent text demonstrates how bad things got. My ex was trying to control my life and weasel out of his responsibilities to the girls and to our divorce decree. He wanted to add a clause in the agreement that would let him off the hook for alimony if I co-habited with Dennis. Naturally, I didn't want to agree to anything so silly, as I had also, over the years compromised on a number of other issues.

Here is the text:

ME: *On my way to a meeting. Whatever you propose put it in writing. Email or text and I will let you know.*

JOHN: *I can't do a deal without a no-cohabitation clause. Between you and my attorney better be honest. Whatever the results on June 23rd (our court date) should anyone move in again, the support will go to zero. It's very likely will be as it stands, so the deal for you, now is good. I strongly suggest having Dennis call your attorney and give him MY fax. Or, call yourself another attorney and give him your fax. Put your meeting off a little bit. Let me know.*

I went to the attorney and he told me to ignore this exchange. John was just trying to bully me into making a bad agreement. A few days later, Sofia had an appointment with a dentist and I sent this:

ME: *There is a copay of $125. Can you please pay for it? I pay for the dental insurance [premiums] through work. It's only fair. Let me know.*

JOHN: (Reply came the next day). *Sent check for Sofia for $75.*

ME: *Thanks.*

JOHN: *Please be aware that I have spent $1000 for Sophia for college and about as much to enroll her is [JC]. Plan B, should they pull her acceptance (which is likely), $200 on her prom, you owe me half for each of those expenses. There will be much more once the accountant is done. Also, [there is the cost of] your child support as of March 30th, 2016 forward. I am also concerned about what's happening when she is with you. Please be positive and kind. This kid was traumatized by YOU. Sorry, but it's true.*

ME: *LOL...you are a prick!*

JOHN: *Your spelling is getting better. Seriously, that is not going to get us anywhere. I'm still open to talk.*

ME: *No.*

JOHN: *That's very unfortunate.*

ME: *From now on, contact your attorney to contact mine. You can contact me only for medical emergencies regarding the girls, please.*

As told to BARBARA RICH

JOHN*: Pride is a killer, Pilar...Seriously. I'll contact you when it's relevant.*
ME*: No, John. You are wrong. Last text please...*

PILAR

As told to BARBARA RICH

Chapter twelve
One Step Forward

There will always be an empty place in the depths of me for my sister's short and tragic life. In the brief span of forty-two years she never had the opportunity to defend herself against the horrors of her childhood. By all standards she should have had a full and happy life. Carmen was beautiful and academically very smart. She had a lot going for her. Unfortunately, instead of benefiting from her many gifts, she was prevented from enjoying her treasures by wounds cast upon her that would never heal. Because she buried her pain so deep, she was swept up in a series of poor decisions that were spawned by circumstances beyond her control. Her self-image spiraled downward to an eternal pit from which she just could not escape.

On the other hand, it will always be a source of joy for me to know that the happiest time in her life was the two weeks she spent with my family in California. I will take those two weeks and keep them safely tucked in my heart forever. My prayer is that she has finally found peace. I think of her often and miss her smile.

My brother Pedro had more opportunities, but again, poor choices led him down a destructive path. Fortunately, he finally escaped the world of drugs, but he did not get the opportunity to live the life he deserved. Destiny had other plans for him. He found himself the guardian for our sister's children and our mother. I am proud of him for being there when he was so desperately needed. Pedro, in his fifties, shouldered the burden of our mother who suffered from Alzheimer's. He could no longer give her the care she needed. Eventually she was placed in a nursing home. The separation anxiety was very difficult for Pedro after all these years. I hope eventually he'll learn to take the opportunity to live a life more self-serving. He sacrificed so much for all of us.

I cannot measure the value of our frequent communication via telephone. We shall continue to love and support each other through our trials. As early as childhood, I knew Pedro would always be there for me.

As told to BARBARA RICH

How often does a day, seeming to be like any other, become something more with the innocent sound of a telephone ringing? I was getting ready for another day I expected would be uneventful, when my brother Pedro called. "Pilar…"

There was a slight moment of silence. I wasn't sure that the connection hadn't been lost, but before I could speak, he finished his sentence. "Papa died, in Colombia this morning."

It took a moment to process and I thought to myself, *my father has been dead to me for decades,* but I asked politely, without emotion, "What happened?"

Pedro went on to explain how the local newspaper had reported our father to be a wonderful man and that he had passed away with "his two sons at his bedside."

"Huh," was all I could say, two sons who I had never even met. In my mind, a flood of memories washed over me. All I could feel was contempt for this man who had brought nothing but pain and misery to my mother and beloved sister.

My father had a total of five—children that we know of--sons out of wedlock, but apparently the paper had only mentioned the two who were still living in Colombia with him. Thank God that he never had any other daughters!

Their mother, Esperanza had moved back to Barcelona with two other illegitimate children. The irony was that my father and Esperanza were never married, because my parents were devoted Catholics, and they would never violate church laws. Naturally, divorce was forbidden, but infidelity and child molestation were considered forgivable infractions.

My mind went to Esperanza for a moment. She had met my father when she was hired as a secretary when he owned a gas station in Colombia. She was young, and my father always seemed to be drawn to younger women.

It was interesting that Pedro was giving me this news without showing any signs of joy or pain. Once, when my father had just started to flaunt his relationship with Esperanza, he boldly paraded her by the front door of our house, the home where he and my mother still officially lived.

As told to BARBARA RICH

My brother Pedro was so incensed that he rushed out of the house and attacked Esperanza with his bare hands! It was a bloody and violent incident, which I'm sure Pedro wanted to forget. It looked to me, as I witnessed this attack that Pedro wanted to kill Esperanza. She ended up in the hospital and took a long time to recover from having her head smashed against the sidewalk.

My father's reaction to this outburst by Pedro was to go into the house and get a gun. He aimed it at Pedro and threatened to kill his only legitimate son. I thought Pedro was a dead man, but something made my father think twice—probably his mind was on the fact that his girlfriend was in need of medical attention-- and he left the room, only to return with a large knife. After threatening both Pedro and my mother for a moment, he rushed out, never to officially return. I suppose I was always grateful that my father did not marry Esperanza, as this would have made her my stepmother!

"Wow," I finally uttered into the telephone. "He got to live a long life with his new family, while my mother continues to suffer and my sister lies in her grave."

PILAR

What else could I feel? What else could I say?

Well, at least my mother didn't have to suffer much longer before complications from breast cancer would take her a year later. Her death, unlike my father's was devastating to me. I suffered and grieved for her a long, long time and still cope with the regret that I could not financially afford to be with her in Barcelona during her last days.

I am not a perfect mother, but what I do correctly is put the welfare of my children above all else. This is true of all good parents, mothers and fathers. It's something I know I learned from my mother and I always tried to show her that I appreciated her great strengths, even in the wake of her glaring weaknesses. One of the things I'll always remember that my mother said to me was, "Bring me flowers while I'm alive."

By this she meant, that we should show our love for one another while it can be appreciated. It is the responsibility of a parent to give the best they can of themselves, for whatever amount of time they are alive, to their children.

As told to BARBARA RICH

I may not have been able to bring her flowers in the way that she wanted me to do, but when I heard of her death, I decided to make an effort to visit her grave with a large bouquet when I first returned to Barcelona where she is now buried. That bouquet, I knew was not for her, but for my sake.

Many memories surrounding her still haunt me today, but I have moved on with some semblance of peace, knowing she suffers no more.

These two were not the only deaths in the litany of losses that I had in a short time. My niece, Carolina called me from London shortly after my mother passed away. She told me that my cousin, Javier had also died suddenly. "It was a heart attack."

A vision of the whole abduction and rape that I'd experienced at his hands escaped from the confines of my mind, where I had locked them away like a wounded animal for these many years. Javier was only fifty-eight, and I was surprised, for some reason by the cause of his demise. I quickly changed the subject. "How have you been?"

PILAR

While Carolina was well aware of what Javier had done to me, she realized that this was not a death I would grieve.

She knew that Javier was one of six cousins on my mother's side. He had never married (no surprise there) and was always on the fringe of the family.

It probably came as no surprise to her that I wanted to change the subject. "Things are going well for me, Tia," she said simply.

She was doing very well, in my eyes and more importantly, in her own. She was a single mother with a wonderful sixteen year-old son, Santiago. We called him Santi.

They were living in London, because Santi wanted to study English in an English speaking country. He was a great student, with very high grades. So, to allow her son the opportunity to pursue his goal, they moved to London.

Carolina had gotten a job in a five star hotel in London, only four days after arriving in England. She is still working there to this day.

Santi now speaks four languages fluently and Carolina, having given birth when she was only a teen, is just thirty-one and still beautiful, and is an excellent mother.

As told to BARBARA RICH

I wished my sister were alive to see how well her daughter had turned out, especially under the difficult circumstances of her early years. I felt a great sense of pride on my sister's behalf.

We spoke in pleasantries for a few more minutes, caught up on what was going on currently in our lives, said goodbye and I hung up the phone.

After my conversation with Carolina, a smile came to my lips as I walked to a nearby cabinet, almost immediately and got a glass. I picked up bottle of wine from the countertop. I loved wine and usually had a glass in the evening to relax at the end of the day, but somehow this did not seem appropriate. I put the bottle back on the counter.

"Screw it!" I thought. "I need something stronger for this." Then, I reached under the sink, finding another bottle of vodka and poured myself a stiff one. I ceremoniously strolled to the sofa and nestled into it. I reviewed that particular, horrific episode in my life, sighed with satisfaction and realized that I am still here. I survived.

There was no love lost between Javier and myself and I celebrated the fact that he could no longer harm me or any one else, ever again. It was the only time in my life I had ever toasted someone's death.

Another tattered and loose end of my past had been cut. There was only one relationship more that I needed to find some sort of completion with. I got that opportunity one night, not long after my divorce was finalized. After I got home from a long day of work, there was a message on my machine from Kitty, my mother-in-law.

The voicemail said that she was sorry for the way her son had treated me. I didn't get back to her until a few days later. There were many times she had called and left no message, and I admit I ignored those calls. This time was different. When I did call her back, we had a very healing conversation, quite out of character with all that had come before. It was a genuine apology on her part. It just goes to show that people can change for the better. It gave me hope.

I felt so comfortable with our communication that I told her about the salad I had made for my ex, her son when I initially heard about his cheating. I don't know why I told her about my revenge, and I questioned my motives as soon as I heard the words coming from my mouth.

"Good for you," was Kitty's response. "He got what he deserved."

After that conversation we become very close. We kept in contact from then on, on a weekly basis. During one of those talks, Kitty told me that she had emphysema and that it was getting worse. My heart went out to her, but she had come to grips with her own trials-of-life. Because of her honesty with herself, she and I had finally become close.

She was eventually hospitalized. Her son and my daughter visited her in the hospital, a few days before she passed away. I was comforted knowing my relationship with her was healed, but I felt a true loss and sadness that Kitty had not known the truth about her son much sooner, which prevented us from developing a truly positive relationship for a longer period.

It was another irony that she died only four days after my own mother. I didn't have to start grieving for my loss from scratch and merely moved from one mother-figure loss to another.

PILAR

As a result of Kitty's death, her other son Ralph started visiting us—especially his nieces. Ralph is not on speaking terms with his brother, my ex-husband. So, basically we are the only family he has left.

Ralph still keeps in close contact with us, checking in to make sure my daughters and I are okay.

As good as John had been with the craziness of my family and helping them throughout the years, as an ex-spouse, all the usual bad traits surfaced.

He is verbally abusive to our girls, just as bad as his mother had been towards everyone. Child support and alimony are constant issues.

Life is quite unique. We never really know how it is going to play out. There is one lesson in all this that drives me forward, motivates me to become a better person and hopefully a better parent: I don't want to die alone.

Luckily, I met a man who wants me to achieve MY goals and lets me know daily that he is never going stand in my way to happiness and healing. I am weary of anyone saying things like, "till death do us part" or "I'll be with you till the end" as that is exactly what my ex told me.

There was a time when John held my hand with all complete sincerity and said, "I will never leave you. I'll always be there for you, and *I will hold your hand, like this till the end.*"

I know, at the time, he meant and believed every word of his pledge. I know he was a good parent in the past, and not a bad person; he was just a person, and people sometimes are overwhelmed by sadness or their own humanness and make promises in the moment that they will never be able to keep.

Dennis never makes unrealistic promises to me, and expects none in return. My relationship with him is growing stronger everyday. I feel I have finally found someone who loves me unconditionally and sets a good example for my children by being a positive male role model in the ways that matter. I now have proof for what I've always believed. Not all men are liars, rapists, pedophiles, or cheaters.

He knows the whole sordid tale of my past and does not hold it against me, or let it affect our relationship. For his calm and honest support of every turn in the bumpy road that I still travel in my life, he will always be a most valued treasure to me, even though sadly…Dennis drinks to excess. We've had long conversations and we both, I believe are clear that I am an alcoholic with other problems. I can't support the overuse of substances, but I am also in no position to judge or offer advice to others right now. He supports my sobriety in all other ways. That's all I need right now.

So, to complete my tale, after long awaiting our trip to Barcelona, my youngest daughter Sofia and I were going to visit my mother's gravesite, unfortunately my oldest daughter, Gabriela couldn't join us because she had just started a new job. She could not get away this soon.

It was not easy to arrange this trip. I was now a single mother, with average wages and was looking forward to my tax refund, which made our trip possible.

But, with all the energy and methodical approach to solving problems that was part of the old Pilar, I dug right in. Soon, before I knew it, everything was ready for our departure. First stop, London.

As told to BARBARA RICH

When we arrived, we went to visit our prearranged lodging and settled in before my family came to visit us. We were so very excited; at least, that was my excuse to myself.

I had been drinking since we left the U.S. After all, I was on vacation, I told myself. That's what ALL adults do on vacation. However, this time, I barely paused between sips. I continued to drink non-stop, one drink after the other, beginning with the flight. Literally, it was like some kind of emotional floodgate was suddenly thrown open.

I must have fallen asleep, because the next thing I knew, I was listening to the flight attendant's landing instructions. I realized we had finally arrived. We were both tired but very excited to see our family.

I can remember, when my family first saw us, we were all thrilled to greet one another and we all went out to dinner, where I continued to drink.

The whole group of us, including the owner of the apartment where we were staying and my brother, Pedro, Carolina, David, Santiago and my daughter, Sofia. It was a local restaurant and we had appetizers. We chatted about our flight and my niece, Carolina was telling us all about London where she was staying.

After dinner Sofia and I returned to our place, as we were exhausted after a long flight and dealing with jet lag.

During the next few days I experienced hangovers, which I took care of with more drinking.

Sofia was spending a lot of time with her cousins while I was either sleeping or drinking.

It never occurred to me that I had a drinking problem. By the end of the week though, I had the shakes so badly, I needed to drink to stop the shaking. I can't even explain the first week I spent there. I was drowning in a sea of alcohol that left me numb.

On Sunday we all went to visit the gravesite of my mother. As I gazed at the gorgeous landscape overlooking the Mediterranean Sea, I thought it was such a peaceful and beautiful final resting place for my mother, whose life had so little peace.

There were no venders selling flowers, so we proceeded by removing flowers from other gravesites. I thought to myself, "They will never know; they are already dead,"

As told to BARBARA RICH

I just couldn't come this far without putting flowers on my mother's grave.

My brother, Pedro watched with anxious eyes as I maneuvered myself out of the back seat and began my ascent to the gravesite. I was very unsteady and I stumbled; Pedro grabbed me so I wouldn't fall and assisted me most of the way because of the many steps and the length of the cemetery to where my mother's gravesite was. I was still witnessing results from my hangover coupled with the heat, which made it difficult for me. I was not very emotional. I did not cry at all. I felt more at peace. "Finally, her suffering was over," is all I kept thinking.

After the visitation at the cemetery we all went out to grab a bite to eat. I must have eaten something, but mostly I resumed my drinking. Unfortunately, I have very little recollection of these days and the days that followed, so I can only piece together with the help of my family what was transpiring. I was in a daze most of the time and missed out on all the things I had wanted to see and do.

Apparently while staying in the apartment we rented, one night I really wanted a cigarette, so I ventured out to one of the other rented rooms where a family from London was staying and I stole a pack of cigarettes. When the landlady found out, she asked me about the incident, but I was so drunk, I fell on top of her. Sofia called my niece, Carolina and told her what happened. Carolina replaced the pack I had stolen and I apologized to the young girl whose cigarettes I had taken.

I had to depend on the reports from my daughter and other members of my family about my outlandish behavior. In addition to theft, I fell down two flights of stairs at my niece's house, which I don't remember. Sofia contacted Dennis, as well as my ex-husband John. They thought I should go to the hospital, but I insisted I was okay. I also tried to pick a fight on the streets of Barcelona, another incident I don't remember. Unfortunately, there are some incidents that I DO recall all too well. Without going into detail, I will say that there was one flight were two totally strange men were treated to the unrestrained version of Pilar. Naturally, alcohol was a factor.

There was the almost two-year period of my life, right after the divorce, where the downward spiral associated with alcohol abuse and depression kept me from functioning at any normal level. My alcohol consumption increased partly because I'd convinced myself that I needed to be relieved from the pain. Then, as it did, I merely became more depressed and angrier. I would stay in bed for days, sometimes weeks at a time, unable to face my own thoughts. For this behavior, I will never be able to apologize enough to my daughters. Without their love and constant urging to "Do something" I might not have survived.

My family did not recognize the Pilar they were seeing. Thank God, my daughter was staying with her cousin and really enjoying herself (I found out later). They went to the beach and visited where I grew up, went shopping, dancing and all the things young girls do on vacation. For the most part my daughter was taking care of me, so I was glad she got to do some fun things.

The night before we were scheduled to return, I bought a bottle of vodka and polished it off. We had to be at the airport at 5a.m. the next day. I woke up and finished packing and left for the airport. We took a taxi and I started to get the shakes again. We had to get in line for the luggage and it just got worse, even my legs were shaking.

Sofia went to the liquor store and purchased a bottle to wine to help me with the shakes. I drank the entire bottle and was able to check our luggage and get on the plane. Once we were on board I made it simple for the flight attendant and asked him to just bring me as many bottles as he could and continued my downward spiral of drinking.

When we arrived back in the U.S., my Gabriela was waiting to pick us up. Sofia had already informed her what had transpired during our visit to Barcelona and it was a tense drive back to our home.

As I had planned ahead, I was able to take a couple more days off before I returned to work. I decided that the time I was waiting for had finally come and I tried to control my drinking on my own, but it was impossible. Somehow I managed to function at work. I was always physically ill and was visibly losing lots of weight. Basically I was skin and bones, due to a combination of vomiting and loss of appetite.

That's when I decided to see a doctor. After a careful review of my symptoms and complaints he ordered the usual tests. After my blood work was returned, they found that my enzymes and cholesterol levels were high and I was anemic. The doctor prescribed some vitamins and told me directly, "Pilar I want you to lower your intake of alcohol."

Of course, I was a little indignant and lied to the doctor about the amount of alcohol I was using. I was slightly relieved that I just needed some vitamins to get me back to normal. Little did I know this was only the beginning of one of the most grueling physical episodes of my life.

Before I went into the hospital, I found that my stomach did not tolerate the vitamins they were giving me, mainly because I wasn't eating hardly any real food and I started to drink even heavier, if you could even imagine that. Dennis was a heavy drinker, also which did not help. It only fueled my temptation and offered me justification to keep drinking on the road to hell.

He would bring large bottles of vodka home, at my request, which we drank together, and this was in addition to my usual intake. Adding fuel to the fire, I also resumed my cigarette habit, yet another addiction. I surely

PILAR

was headed in what seemed to be an inescapable downward spiral.

Working became more and more difficult because of my declining health. I remember is was my daughter, Gabriela's birthday, but I was so sick, I had to call Dennis and ask him to pick me up from work. He took me home, but he wanted to take me to the hospital.

In my mind I was thinking, "No, I can't go. What if they find some horrible terminal disease? Maybe, I'm dying. I'm too scared."

When we got home I had the shakes so bad, I needed a drink, but nothing would stay down, I kept gagging because there was no food in me.

I called Ralph who knew of my drinking problem and explained how I was feeling.

"Pilar, if you need me to take you to the hospital let me know" he offered.

"Ralph," I answered, "let me call you back later. I will see how I'm feeling then."

My hand was trembling so bad I could barely even hang up the phone. When I turned around from the wall where the phone hung, Dennis was watching. I started to wretch again. His eyes were wide and full of concern as he said, "Pilar, I've got to get you to the hospital. Please, let's go now."

Upon arriving at the ER, a full blood panel was taken. I was so sick; I just wanted to feel normal again. Finally, the doctor came in. He didn't have the best bedside manner. He looked at me and asked, "Pilar, have you been drinking?"

I answered honestly, and simple said, "Yes."

The doctor glanced down at the blood results, flipped a few pages on my charts and said, "You have extreme inflammation of the pancreas and you will need to be admitted to the hospital immediately." He left the room then, I assume to make preparations for me to be admitted.

In the meantime Dennis texted Sofia and briefly told her what was happening. Sofia came to the hospital as soon as she could. Once I was settled in my hospital room with two IVs and an assortment of meds, Dennis and my daughter came in to see me.

After a short while, the doctor reentered. He observed Dennis and Sofia, he then turned to me and asked, "May I speak candidly in the presence of your daughter?" I looked over at Sofia and felt that she should hear whatever he had to say. She would find out eventually anyway, if she already didn't know.

"Yes, you can speak freely with both Dennis and Sofia present."

The doctor addressed Sofia and said with as little emotion possible, "Your mother is in very bad shape physically. I have reviewed the results of her tests and based upon her current condition and apparent lifestyle choices, I give her three months to live."

My heart quickened when I saw the expression on Sofia's face. I was more crushed by her reaction than the actual prognosis. There was silence and nobody spoke for a moment. I watched the tears stream down Sofia's face as she came towards me. I also realized that Gabriela had not heard yet and I would have to go through this emotion at least one more time.

I was so weak, emotionally and physically I just wanted to give up, but that was not in my nature. I had been through so much in my life and overcame so many obstacles placed before me. I knew that I am not a quitter and resolved right then to beat death—or at least hold it off for longer than three months--for my daughters, if not for my own sake. I just had to survive!

I was in and out of awareness for a few days, but the surprises kept coming. I remember slowly awakening, shortly after I was told I probably would die soon and seeing a person—blurry image at first, coming slowly into focus—standing right next to my bed. It was John. He had pulled a chair around in front of him as if he were standing in a courtroom rather than by a sick person's bedside.

"What are you doing here?" I asked.

As soon as he realized I was coherent, he said, "I think this is a good time for us to discuss the future of the girls and selling the house. I heard you are not going to survive."

Even in my numb state, I could not believe the insensitivity. All I could say, before turning my face away from him was, "This is NOT a good time. You need to leave." He left.

All of a sudden, I wanted a cigarette so badly that the thought was overpowering all else, even the pronouncement of my impending death or my anger at John.

So, in a matter of minutes, I went into the restroom and was smoking a cigarette. This is not as easy as it sounds, since I was

PILAR

handicapped with two IVs, a heart monitor, a blood pressure cuff and a finger clamp to monitor (ironically) my oxygen level.

I thought that no one would know, since I hadn't seen a nurse for over an hour and the doctor had probably told the nurses to give me some space. However, I soon found out the beds in the hospital have an alarm that is triggered when a patient gets up unexpectedly. By my second drag, I heard the nurse's voice outside the door. "You can't smoke in the hospital. You could blow up the hospital with all the oxygen and other chemicals. Please come out."

Opening the door sheepishly I said, "I'm sorry." I was feeling guilty. "I just wanted a cigarette. It won't happen again," I added.

My words were sincere when they came out of my mouth. After I thought about it, I really didn't want to put anyone's life in danger, but I still wanted a cigarette. When the need for another cigarette swept over me, I abandoned my promise and started to plan my next move.

After some trial and error, I figured out, in an hour or so, how to disconnect the alarm on the bed and started to plan my escape down the elevator (two levels), walked past the reception desk, and went outside to smoke another cigarette.

It's amazing what you can do when you are desperate. I watched carefully for the right moment, and made my way down the elevator to the first floor and out the door. Once outside, I hid as best I could behind a bush while dragging my IVs and connected tubes behind me. With some guilt I smoked my cigarette. Managing this all without anyone questioning or trying to stop me.

Obviously smoking was not even permitted in the parking lot. There are very strict regulations at the hospital. Nevertheless, I continued my escapades of smoking about three times a day.

Honestly, that is one of the most eventful parts of my stay in the hospital, along with the scheduled meds and tests. Eventually I confessed to my doctor about my smoking habit and he pronounced quickly, "Pilar, cigarettes may kill you one day, but continuing to drink will kill you ***right now***. If you have to keep one terrible habit, between the two, for now…just don't drink, and please don't tell me about this again."

PILAR

After eleven days in the hospital, I was finally released. I was given an extensive list of do's and don'ts, which I followed strictly, determined to turn my life around. In fact the same day I was released, I had a sincere desire, which was very unfamiliar to me. I wanted to go to an AA meeting.

I still was not feeling that great, so I asked my daughter, Gabriela if she would take me to a meeting that night.

"This is one of the best things you've ever asked of me," she said.

An old friend I had known for years (an AA member) was going to meet me there, so I felt comfortable. She was experienced in helping others to stay sober so she didn't make anything of the fact that it was an important first step.

I did not share that evening, but I felt better knowing that I'd taken this important step to a more healthy life, by admitting that I had a problem and that I was powerless to defeat my demons without sober support.

I continued attending these meetings twice a day for thirty days, decreasing that time to once a day after that. Ten days after my release from the hospital I returned to work feeling the healing process was taking hold. I was determined to make a better life for myself, and my family.

It is probably not necessary to describe in detail my first meetings or what I heard or shared there. After listening to other people's stories, my problems were being put into a manageable context.

Though there are always low points in life, and certainly things would be better in many ways, I believe, overall, I am doing well because I have no desire to have a drink. I can be around others who are drinking alcohol without that feverish desire to join them. This new perspective has only come about recently. Remember, this book took seven years to finish. Most of the people mentioned here are either gone or grown. The most important thing for me now, is that I'm still alive. The doctor's prediction did not come true!

It may be that my drinking was an escape from the other memories that had haunted me for so long. I wonder. Maybe somewhere in this question is just one more of those important life lessons. It doesn't cause panic anymore for me to wonder about the thoughts hidden behind my actions. I move forward now to heal and restore my body and mind.

Life often seems to happen all around us, but we certainly need to take responsibility for our part in it. We just can't base our happiness on how little or how much others might take or avoid responsibility. This is something that I've learned from twelve step programs. I am working on becoming more honest with myself, on cleaning up the wreckage of my life, which I have the power to do.

What is equally important is that I remember that sometimes WE ARE THE WRECKAGE of someone else's life, but most of the time people just keep moving forward and never go back to make amends.

I didn't want my daughters, or anyone else, to become my wreckage! I had spent a lifetime blocking out what I felt were the horrors that others had inflicted on me, without realizing that pushing memories or feelings into the blackness, doesn't make them go away. They still are there and can only be conquered in the light of sober, honest awareness.

I know that there are people reading this right now who are rolling their eyes and thinking, "This alcoholic has been brainwashed by therapy and Twelve Step programs. Every other word out of her mouth comes right out of a Big Book somewhere." I know that this kind of self-reflection is not for everyone, and I respect that, but I also know that at a point in my life, my brain really needed washing.

Right before I hit bottom, everyone thought I should go to the hospital, but I insisted I was okay. There are many incidents, after and before what is written here, that may be part of other writing someday...maybe not. What has happened before, or even what might come after today, is not as important as this moment, right now, this one day. Living in the moment, I'm told, is the only way to stay sane. Some have even said that wisdom is measured by this ability.

Life goes on, with our without my sobriety, for everyone. I can only do my best to make the best decisions and choices I can, based upon what I know to be healthful for both me and my family, such as picking the right people to associate with.

My relationships with my daughters and with Dennis are good examples of the new me that I'd like to become. I want to be proud of the choices I make, and pick people to share my

PILAR

time with based upon good character and honesty. These are not unrealistic expectation for human beings. I do not apologize for these choices.

Everyone has their own demons to conquer; I also know that I'm a seriously handicapped work-in-progress. Like every person on the planet, even my best intentions will always be slightly painted with the color of self-doubt and deep-seated learned behavior. After all, I know that I can repress negative thoughts and memories as well as anyone, but there will always be a consequence.

Almost daily there is a new tiny piece of memory that surfaces, and then there is always the heavy drinking period of my life where I know I did things that I am not proud of, but that does not change the responsibilities I now feel I've accepted to live a better, healthier life. Since change is inevitable and my story, like everyone else is continually being rewritten based upon new recollections or changes in perspective, I better end it here with one thing that keeps me moving forward: There is no reason to worry about the past. We can never change it, but we can make decisions now that will make us proud to be who we are. I know

As told to BARBARA RICH

there is still a lot of work that I must do, and many things I still need to learn as I do the hard work to become a Pilar I can be proud of.

PILAR

As told to BARBARA RICH

Photo Album

Our Mother

Angel

As told to BARBARA RICH

Pedro dances with Carmen

PILAR

Pilar and Pedro

As told to BARBARA RICH

Carmen, Pedro, Pilar

PILAR

www.ingramcontent.com/pod-product-compliance
Lightning Source LLC
Chambersburg PA
CBHW020611300426
44113CB00007B/599